Throwing the

Perfect

Party

Laci and Baby

Throwing the Perfect Party

Fun Games & Activities for Wedding & Baby Showers

Jill Williams Grover

Sterling Publishing Co., Inc. New York

A Sterling/Chapelle Book

Chapelle, Ltd., Inc.

P.O. Box 9252, Ogden, UT 84409
(801) 621-2777 • (801) 621-2788 Fax
e-mail: chapelle@chapelleltd.com
Web site: www.chapelleltd.com

Library of Congress Cataloging-in-Publication Data

Grover, Jill Williams.
  Throwing the perfect party : fun games & activities for wedding
& baby showers / Jill Williams Grover.
        p. cm.
  Includes index.
  ISBN 1-4027-1227-8
1. Showers (Parties) 2.   Indoor games. I. Title.

GV1472.7.S5G75 2005
793.2–dc22
                                                    2005001197

10 9 8 7 6 5 4 3 2 1
Published by Sterling Publishing Co., Inc.
387 Park Avenue South, New York, NY 10016
©2005 by Jill Williams Grover
Distributed in Canada by Sterling Publishing
c/o Canadian Manda Group, 165 Dufferin Street
Toronto, Ontario, Canada M6K 3H6
Distributed in Great Britain by Chrysalis Books Group PLC,
The Chrysalis Building, Bramley Road, London W10 6SP, England
Distributed in Australia by Capricorn Link (Australia) Pty. Ltd.
P. O. Box 704, Windsor, NSW 2756, Australia
Printed and Bound in China
All Rights Reserved

Sterling ISBN 1-4027-1227-8

    For information about custom editions, special sales, premium
and corporate purchases, please contact Sterling Special Sales
Department at 800-805-5489 or specialsales@sterlingpub.com.

Space would not permit the inclusion of every decorative item photographed for this book, nor could all of the designers be identified. Many of these items are available by contacting:

  Ruby & Begonia
  204 25th Street, Ogden, UT 84401
  (801) 334-7829 • (888) 888-7829 Toll-free
  e-mail: ruby@rubyandbegonia.com
  Web site: www.rubyandbegonia.com

    Every effort has been made to ensure that all information in this book is accurate. However, due to differing conditions, tools, and individual skills, the publisher cannot be responsible for any injuries, losses, and/or other damages which may result from the use of the information in this book.

    This volume is meant to stimulate craft ideas. If readers are unfamiliar or not proficient in a skill necessary to attempt a project, we urge that they refer to an instructional book specifically addressing the required technique.

My Happily Ever After!

Introducing the newest member
of my family–Navi Jill . . .
my inspiration.

Introduction

Throwing the Perfect Party will help you with the games and activities that make a wedding or baby shower not only fun, but also memorable.

Both the wedding and baby shower chapters offer five complete parties that have been created around individual themes. Each outlines the party, including its theme, invitation, menu, and an activity or game specific to the theme. Each section also includes additional games and activities that can be adapted to your celebration, regardless of the theme.

Enjoy!

Jill W. Grover

Contents

Wedding Showers 8

Baby Showers 62

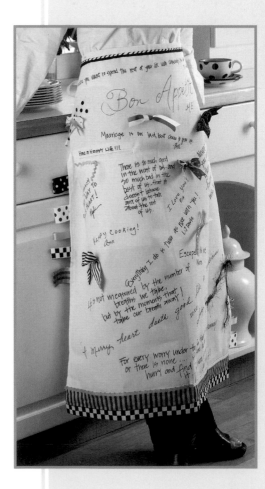

Wedding Showers

Instead of a traditional shower, plan a girl's day out filled with pampering and shopping for the bride-to-be and a few special guests.

Stop & Smell the Roses

Preparation

What You Need

• A boxed lunch for each guest with food and drinks listed in the Menu on page 12

• A card for all the guests to sign

• A fancy purse for the bride-to-be

• A rented limousine and driver

• A rose bouquet for the bride-to-be

• A single rose for each guest

• Decorations as described on page 13

• Invitation supplies as described on page 12

What To Do Ahead

Plan the guest list based on how many people can comfortably ride in the limousine.

Stop & Smell the Roses

It's a Girls' Day Out!

For:

Date:

Time:

Place:

RSVP:

Join us in helping the bride-to-be leave her wedding worries behind by taking time out to stop and smell the roses. We will be having a light lunch and going on a shopping trip.

Please bring a cash amount to contribute to the bride-to-be's gift. No other gift is necessary.

Invitation

Copy the artwork at upper left onto the right side of a paper cut twice as wide as the card front. Fold the paper into a card. On the inside, copy the invitation information at lower left.

This shower is best for inviting the wedding party, a few close friends, or family members.

Menu

Girl-friendly Veggie Wraps

Giant Strawberries with Raspberry Dip

Yummy Chocolate Chip Scones

Rose Petal Cookies

Beautiful Bottle of Water

Rose Petal Cookies

⅓ c shortening

1 c white sugar

2 eggs

1 tsp rose fluid (available from many drugstores)

2 c flour

¼ tsp salt

Red decorator's sugar

Mix shortening, sugar, eggs and rose fluid until fluffy. Stir flour and salt together, then mix in shortening mixture. Dough will be soft. Chill several hours or overnight.

Preheat oven to 350 degrees. Lightly grease cookie sheets.

Using one third of the dough at a time (keeping the rest refrigerated), roll into ¾" balls. Place on cookie sheets. Flatten balls with your hand until they are approximately half their original thickness. Using a knife, make two slits, each ½" long, in each cookie at 10 o'clock and at 2 o'clock. Pinch the bottom to form the "base" of the petal. Sprinkle with red decorator's sugar.

Bake for 8 to 10 minutes or until lightly browned on the bottom.

Decorations

🎁 Add a special touch to the boxed lunches by decorating each box. Wrap shoe boxes in fancy paper. Wrap the lid separately so that it can be removed without disturbing the wrapping. Decorate the boxes with silk roses to match the theme of the party and tie with bridal tulle. Slip a name card for each guest under the tulle. Use small take-out boxes to hold Rose Petal Cookies. Matching cloth toile napkins crown the ensemble, epitomizing the luxury of the day.

🎁 Arrange to have the limousine and driver arrive before the shower begins so you can personalize your trip by stocking the wet bar with bottles of champagne, color-coordinated napkins, and matching containers filled with

hors d'oeuvres and sweet treats. Create a seating arrangement by placing the boxed lunches with name cards on the seats where you would like the guests and the bride-to-be to sit. Supply the driver with roses to give the guests and bride-to-be.

Activity

🎁 When all of the guests have arrived, seat them in the limousine and have the driver give each person a rose. Collect the money from each guest and place it in a fancy purse selected for the honoree. Have all the guests sign the card and slip it into the purse as well. After everyone is settled, have the driver escort the bride-to-be to the limousine and present her with a rose bouquet. As a group, present the bride-to-be with the purse full of money.

The limousine will take the group to the bride's favorite shopping place(s). En route, guests can enjoy drinks, hors d'oeuvres, and box lunches previously stored in the car.

More Activities

🎁 While traveling to the shopping center, play "I have never … ." Guests dig into their purses and take out a specific number of coins. (You may want to ask each guest to come prepared with a roll of quarters). Each guest then takes a turn confessing a particular thing they have never done such as, "I have never been on a blind date." Each guest that has done that particular thing puts one of her coins in a small piggy bank. When someone is out of coins the game ends. The guest with the most coins left is the winner. With the collected money, purchase a small gift for the bride while shopping.

Favors

🎁 Along with the personalized boxes and roses, you could favor your guests with small rose-scented perfume samples as a reminder of this precious time spent together.

This shower centers around the kitchen. The activity will help the new bride add favorite family recipes to her collection.

Cookbook Shower

Preparation

What You Need

• A blank recipe book

• Blank recipe cards

• Decorations as described on page 19

• Fine-tipped markers, pens, a variety of ribbons, stickers, and embellishments

• Invitation supplies as described on page 18

• Permanent fabric markers

• Two white aprons

What To Do Ahead

If the recipe book cover is blank, decorate it with the markers and embellishments.

COOK
BOOK

...Ben ph...
...ge is our last, best ch...
...e is so much good...
...the worst of th...

Lemon frosting—
¼ TB Butter
4½ cups confectioners' sugar
About ½ cup Heavy Cream
1½ TB vanilla extract
1 fresh

Party Popovers

In the ba
electric
On low.
sugar.
Beat unt

1¼ cup flour
¼ salt
3 large eggs
1¼ cup milk
2 TBs butter
oil Popover Pan. Preheat
set rack in oven

(Bride's Name) Surprise

Ingredients:

15 friends

1 bride-to-be

1 favorite recipe from each friend

On   (date)   at   (time)   collect in 1 warm kitchen at (address)   for 1 kitchen shower. Mix together. Simmer and mingle for a culinary night of fun for the bride-to-be.

Please bring a 3" x 5" card with the recipe for making your favorite dish!

Invitation

🎁 Copy the recipe card above, masking off the words in parentheses, then write in the specific information in the spaces provided.

More Invitation Ideas

🎁 You may want to request favorite recipes in specific categories such as appetizers, salads, main courses, and desserts so that the new bride doesn't get 15 recipes for brownies—though that may not be such a bad thing!

🎁 To accompany the recipes, suggest that each guest also bring the ingredients required for making her favorite dish to give to the bride-to-be.

Menu

🎁 Arrange a potluck dinner by having each guest bring the cooked dish that she selected for her recipe. Make certain to assign an appetizer, a salad, a main dish or two, and a few desserts.

🎁 Serve fruit juices, fresh fruits in season, and fresh croissants to accompany the food items contributed by the guests.

Decorations

🎁 Make place mats for the guests by decorating a recipe card with a favorite recipe and enlarging it.

🎁 When serving, use pint jars as drink glasses, pie tins as plates, and terra cotta saucers as chargers.

Make a centerpiece for the table, filling tissue paper-lined terra cotta pots with breadsticks, cookies, and sweets. Fill tall glass bottles and vases with fresh flowers. Wrap juice carafes in cloth napkins and embellish with glass fruit pins.

Favors

Place kitchen-themed stickers under several of the guests' chairs. When the party is over, have your guests check their chairs. Those with stickers get to take home selected decoration items.

Tie a ribbon around a small cheese grater with a tag attached that reads, "It was 'grate' having you here with us to celebrate (bride's name) wedding."

Activities

🎁 During the shower, all guests sit together at a work table and write their favorite recipe on a recipe card. They then decorate their recipe card with stickers, embellishments, or individual drawings. Each guest then adheres her own card onto a blank page in the blank recipe book. She selects a ribbon that will remind the bride-to-be of the "author" and adheres it to the side of the page that has her recipe. The ribbon will then act as a divider or a bookmark.

Have extra recipe cards on hand in the event guests want a copy of someone else's recipe.

🎁 Have each guest sign her name and best wishes onto each of the two aprons with a permanent fabric marker. One apron should be addressed to the bride and the other should be addressed to the groom. He, of course, will want to take his turn in the kitchen and should not feel that he doesn't have a very "special" apron of his own to wear while cooking!

More Activities

🎁 Play the Bride's Menu game. Hand out a worksheet to each guest. Each guest lists the top 10 meals she thinks the bride-to-be will cook first and in order. The bride-to-be also makes a list. The guest who matches the bride the most wins. The prize could be a gift certificate for a specified amount to be spent at a cooking implements store.

Copy this worksheet so there are enough for each guest attending the shower. Provide pens for filling in the answers.

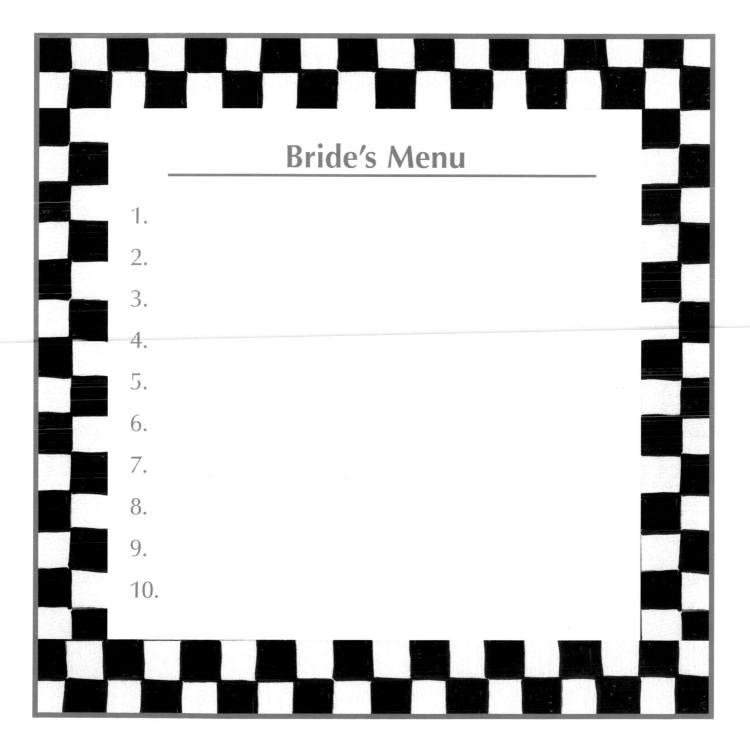

Bride's Menu

1.

2.

3.

4.

5.

6.

7.

8.

9.

10.

Find out where the bride and groom are going to honeymoon and throw a party celebrating the couple's trip. For example, if the couple is going to Hawaii, have a luau.

Honeymoon Shower

Preparation

What You Need

- A large beach bag

- A large handkerchief for each guest to be included with their invitation

- A new themed suitcase

- Decorations as described on pages 24–25

- Food and drinks listed in the Menu on page 24

- Invitation supplies as described on page 24

- Several small plastic fish

Here today, gone to Maui!

For:
Date:
Time:
Place:
RSVP:

Come enjoy a tropical island afternoon for the bride and groom!

Please bring a small gift wrapped in the enclosed handkerchief to match the theme, such as tanning lotion, lip balm, sunglasses, a disposable camera, a bikini or swim trunks; or more generic must-have items for the honeymoon, such as breathmints, bubblebath, lingerie, etc.

Please also bring a desired money amount in one-dollar bills.

Invitation

📖 Copy the artwork at upper left onto the right side of a paper cut twice as wide as the card front. Fold the paper into a card. On the inside, copy the invitation information at lower left.

Menu

Island Lime Shrimp

Maui Rice

Fruit Kabobs with Mango Sauce

Tropical Island Pineapple Cake

Sunshine Swizzle Punch

Fruit Kabobs with Mango Sauce

6 c of assorted fruit, cut into bite-size pieces

1 c green or red grapes

1 c berries of choice

3 small star fruit, cut into 24 slices

2 large mangoes, peeled, pitted, cut into large pieces

¼ c pineapple preserves

Thread four to six pieces of fruit (except mangoes) on each of twenty-four 6" skewers. Place skewers on large Hawaiian serving platter; set aside.

Place mango pieces and pineapple preserves in food processor. Cover and process until smooth; pour into a small serving bowl.

Decorations

📖 Decorate to match the theme. Create a centerpiece with tropical flowers and leaves. Line the walkway outside your home with tiki torches. Use hula skirts to skirt the serving and gift tables. Mount beach towels on the walls or lay them out on the floor for guests to sit on. Hang up travel posters. Fill large glass vases or bowls with seashells. Have Hawaiian music playing in the background.

More Ideas

Have the guests come dressed in attire that the bride and groom will see on their honeymoon, such as Hawaiian-themed shirts or in "obvious" travel clothes. During the party, cast votes for which guests are the best and worst dressed for the trip.

Greet each guest at the door with a themed surprise, such as a silk or authentic floral lei.

Activities

As the guests arrive, collect their handkerchief-wrapped items and place them in the themed suitcase prominently displayed in the room.

During the party have everyone sit down and have the bride and groom choose one handkerchief at a time and try to guess what is wrapped inside. Have the couple bestow a tropical wish upon the gift-givers before opening the gift. Once everything is open, the couple has a suitcase full of "important" items to take on the trip.

Make a money lei for the couple to take on the trip. Fold one-dollar bills in half. Using a needle and a strand of monofilament long enough to create a long necklace, pierce the center of a folded dollar bill and string each onto the strand until it is filled. Space the folded bills with beads and silk flowers and leaves. Tie the ends of the strand together. Present it to the honored couple.

Place several small plastic fish with two or three marked as winners in a beach bag. Have guests take turns reaching into the bag and "fishing" one out.

More Activities

🎁 Sell raffle tickets for whatever amount you think is appropriate for your guest list. The money collected for the tickets is put in a piggy bank and then given to the couple for their honeymoon. The raffle prize should be something that represents where the couple is going to for their honeymoon.

🎁 Play The Letter Game. Provide a large potato-style sack for each guest—these could be made from tropical-print fabrics. Have the guests sit on the floor in their sacks. Hold up a letter at random. The first one to stand up in their sack and shout something that begins with that letter that best describes their partner, wins the card. For example, "L" = Lazy and "S" = Sexy. The one with the most cards when all the cards are held up wins.

Prizes & Favors

🎁 Appropriate game prizes and favors for this themed shower would be items such as those brought for the suitcase activity—sunglasses, tanning lotion, flip-flops, or something more tropical such as a coconut or a fresh pineapple.

Enlarge and copy this worksheet once and cut out each letter. Arrange the letters in a pile randomly so the guests cannot think ahead of the game.

The Letter Game

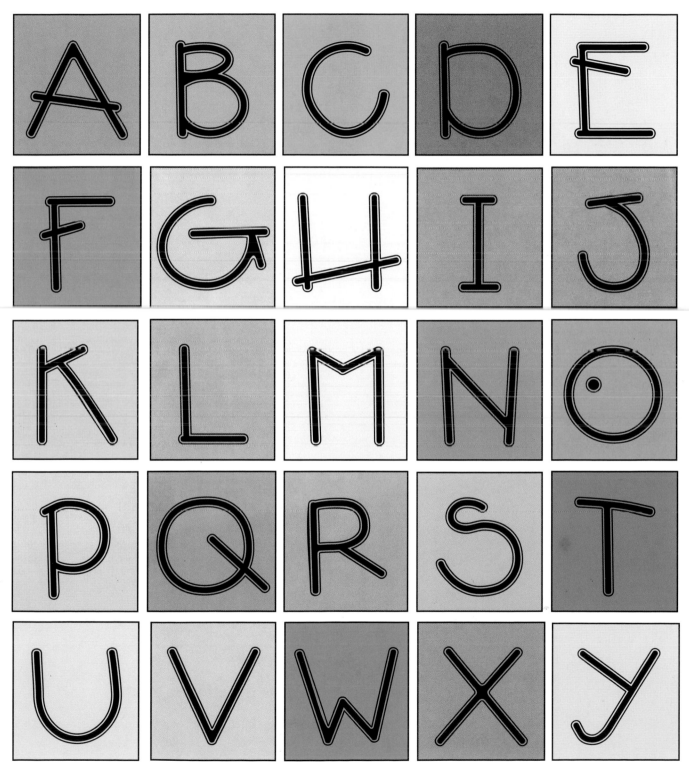

Celebrating a couple's first date and first song is certain to bring back fond memories for the honored couple.

They're Playing Our Song

Preparation

What You Need

- 45 RPM vintage records

- Art chalks, crayons, markers, water paints

- Blank CDs and CD cases

- Copies of Couples' Songs worksheet on page 33

- Decorations as described on pages 30–31

- Food and drinks listed in the Menu on page 30

- Glossy paper cut to fit CD cases

- Invitation supplies as described on page 30

What To Do Ahead

Make Record Album Bowls for the guests as favors following instructions on page 32.

Invitation

🎁 Copy the invitation at right for each couple on the guest list. Using light-colored ink, write in the appropriate date, time, and place information. Personalize the outside rim of the record with the names of the bride- and groom-to-be and write in any other necessary information.

Menu

Shrimp in Love Pasta

"Hot Dates"

Honey-glazed Pecans

They're Playing Our Song Salad

Tie the Knot Pretzels

Sweetheart Tarts

Passion Punch

Hot Dates

1 pkg (8 oz.) pitted dates

30 shelled pecan halves

12 slices bacon

Preheat oven to 400 degrees. Presoak toothpicks in water so they don't burn in oven.

Set a rack in broiler 6" from the heat source. Place a pecan in each date. Cut each slice of bacon in half, wrap one around each stuffed date, and secure with a toothpick. Broil 12 to 15 minutes until

Love Song

Date:

Time:

Place:

bacon is crisp. Drain dates on a paper towel. Serve while still warm.

Serving Tip: Serve these dates on a skinny slip of paper that says "Hot Dates." Leave 3" blank on paper, then write the words "Hot Dates." Place the date on the blank paper so guests can see the words.

Decorations

🎁 Purchase vintage record albums and place them about the party room. Hang records or CDs from the ceiling by attaching a long strand of transparent monofilament thread to each and securing it to the ceiling with a push pin. Use 33 rpm record discs as

plate chargers. Have the centers cut from other records and use them as coasters.

Activities

- As guests arrive, hand out the Couples' Songs worksheets and have each couple fill in the blanks, writing down the song from their first dance plus the name of their favorite love song. The bride- and groom-to-be should write the name of the song to which they first danced and the first song they will dance to as a married couple. When everyone is finished, gather the worksheets.

During the party, the guests are seated and given a small notebook. The hostess reads the names of the songs written down by each couple (numbered 1 and 2 on the worksheet—do not include the songs written by the honored couple at this time); each couple makes a list of the songs, then confers and writes down who in the room they believe chose those two songs. Guests then guess the two songs the bride- and groom-to-be wrote down. The hostess

then reads the answers. Guests receive one point for each correct guess and five points if they guess the honored couple's songs. For fun, the bride- and groom-to-be can take turns reading the other answers guests provided on their worksheets.

- Give guests blank pieces of glossy paper, cut to fit a CD case. Supply them with crayons, markers, water paints, chalks, etc. Have each couple design their own love song album cover. When everyone is finished with their design, hang them up for display throughout the rest of the party.

Prizes

- Award the winner a CD of love songs or a gift certificate for a new CD from a music store.

More Activities

- Play your own version of "name that tune." Create a CD by copying a few notes of a number of love songs your guests would be familiar with. The player who can name that tune first wins a point. The player with the most points wins a musical gift.

- To find out even more about the bride- and groom-to-be, invite the groom to your home in advance and video-tape his version of their first date. In a separate interview, invite the bride and tape her version. Ask questions such as "How did you first meet?", "When and where was your first date?", "Who asked who out?", "What did each of you wear?", "When did you hold hands first?", "How long until the groom called the bride after the first date?" Have the entire video playing while the food is served.

🎁 Play musical chairs. Place guests' chairs in a circle. Remove one chair so there is one less chair than the number of guests. Play a selection of love songs while guests move around the circle. When you stop the music, guests must take a seat. The guest without a seat is out of the game. Remove another chair and continue play in this manner until there is one chair and one winner.

🎁 Rent or borrow a karaoke machine. Have guests take turns selecting a song to sing for the rest of the group. Hand out slips of paper for guests to cast votes for the best and worst performances.

🎁 Play "Pass It On." In two small lingerie-type boxes, place a small but nice-to-wear item—one for a woman and one for a man—such as a necklace, a watch, a silk scarf or necktie, etc. Label the boxes "male" and "female."

Tell the guests that you are going to start some music and pass around the boxes. When the music stops, the boxes stop with the closest male or female guest. Whoever has a box must put on whatever is in the box. The guests are likely to panic, thinking it is lingerie, but it will actually be a very nice surprise.

Favors

🎁 If you have computer access to a music store via the Internet, have someone not attending the shower take the list of songs from the Couples' Songs activity and download all of the songs into his music player while you continue with the rest of the shower. Once the songs are downloaded, he can burn them onto CDs and print a list of the songs for each couple to take home. Have each couple insert their own love song album cover into the CD case.

🎁 Make a record album bowl as a party favor for each guest.

Record Album Bowls

What you need:
Cookie sheets
Oven
Oven-safe bowls
45 RPM vintage record albums

What to do:
Preheat oven to 200 degrees, place record on top of an oven-safe bowl that is turned upside down. Place bowl on a cookie sheet for ease when moving in and out of oven. Bake for 3–5 minutes until record forms around the bowl. Remove and allow to cool.

Note: Make certain guests understand these bowls are to be used only for dry food items such as chips and pretzels. They will need to take the time to line them with a food-safe plastic bowl or plastic wrap before using them for other types of food.

Copy this worksheet so there are enough for each couple attending the shower. Provide pens with light-colored ink for filling in the answers.

Couples' Songs

1. What is your "song?"

2. What song did you and your spouse or date dance to first?

3. What is the honored couple's favorite love song?

Play Our Song Again

4. What song did the honored couple dance to first?

5. What is the first song the honored couple will dance to after they are married?

6. What humorous song could reflect the type of relationship the honored couple has had?

This themed party plays on the words "Great Pair," using pears or pairs in the decorations, foods, and gifts.

What a Great Pair

Preparation

What You Need

• Copies of A Great Pair worksheet on page 39

• Decorations as described on page 36

• Food and drinks listed in the Menu on page 37

• Glitter

• Invitation supplies as described on page 36

• Paper or plastic pears

• Silk wedding flowers

• Spray adhesive

• Transparent stickers

What To Do Ahead

Have the bride- and groom-to-be answer worksheet questions.

A Great Pair

Help us celebrate the great pair!

For: (bride) and (groom)
Date:
Time:
Place:

Please bring a "pair" of something for the couple to enjoy such as a pair of tickets to a sporting event, his and hers towels, a pair of wine glasses, etc.

Invitation

📦 Copy the artwork above onto the right side of a paper cut twice as wide as the card front. Fold the paper into a card. On the inside, copy the invitation information above, masking off words in parentheses.

Decorations

📦 Hang two perfect pears from a purchased wreath with a pretty ribbon. Place it at the front door to greet guests. Nestle pears in sets of two randomly about the house.

📦 For the centerpiece, place a platter on the table. Arrange fresh pears on the platter. To make certain the pears will stand upright, cut a thin slice off of the bottom. Cut a hole through the stem end of the fruit with an apple corer. Slide a candle into the hole. Place a pair of pear-scented candles at each place setting.

📦 Place black-and-white photos of famous couples around the room. Include a photo of the bride- and groom-to-be in the selection.

Chilled Pear Soup

Great Pear Salad

Pleasing Pair of Croissants

Puffed Pear Tartlet A la Mode

Blushing Pear Spritzer

Great Pear Salad
Dressing
½ c oil

3 Tbl apple cider vinegar

¼ c sugar

½ tsp celery seed

¼ tsp salt

Combine all ingredients in a jar with a tight lid. Shake well until sugar is dissolved and the dressing is blended. Refrigerate.

Salad
2 heads butter lettuce, torn into pieces

2 pears, cored and chopped

½ c toasted walnuts

3 oz. blue cheese, crumbled

Combine all salad ingredients and toss with dressing just before serving. Serves 6.

Activities

🎁 Make pear place-card holders for the wedding dinner to help the bride with her wedding decorations. Take plastic or paper pears, spray with adhesive, then roll each pear in glitter. Have the couple's names or a favorite quote preprinted on transparent stickers and add to the pear. Cut a slit in the top of the pear for the name tag, adhere the bride's wedding flower to the top.

🎁 Play the A Great Pair game. Hand out A Great Pair worksheets. Have couples work together in pairs. Have each pair (including the bride- and groom-to-be) answer as many questions about the bride and groom as possible in the allotted amount of time. When the time is finished, the bride and groom read their answers. The pair with the most matches wins a prize that is a pair of something such as two tickets to the local movie theater.

More Activities

🎁 Hand out disposable cameras to each guest as they arrive at the shower, with a tag attached that says "Take the goofiest picture of a pair" meaning any of the couples invited to the party.

Have the pictures developed, then make the bride and groom an album with these pictures on the first page. The album could be pair themed and different ideas could be added to the individual pages for the new couple to add to as they wish.

🎁 Play the Famous Pairs Match Up game. Copy the worksheet below. Have guests match the pairs between the lists. The most correct answers wins.

Famous Pairs Match Up

1. Abelard	a. Annie Oakley
2. Abraham	b. Bathsheba
3. Adam	c. Blondie
4. Ahasuerus	d. Carol
5. Anthony	e. Cleopatra
6. Boaz	f. Daisy
7. Dagwood	g. Delilah
8. David	h. Elizabeth
9. Donald	i. Esther
10. Frank Butler	j. Eve
11. Isaac	k. Heloise
12. Jacob	l. Mary
13. Joseph	m. Minnie
14. Mickey	n. Olive Oil
15. Mike Brady	o. Queen Victoria
16. Moses	p. Rachael
17. Popeye	q. Rebekah
18. Prince Albert	r. Ruth
19. Robert Browning	s. Sarah
20. Samson	t. Zipporah

Answers: 1. k, 2. s, 3. j, 4. i, 5. e, 6. r, 7. c, 8. b, 9. f, 10. a, 11. q, 12. p, 13. i, 14. m, 15. d, 16. t, 17. n, 18. o, 19. h, 20. g

Copy this worksheet so there are enough for each couple attending the shower. Provide pens for filling in the answers.

A Great Pair

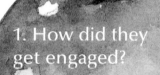

1. How did they get engaged?

2. Where are they going for their honeymoon?

3. Where did they meet?

4. Where was their first date?

5. Where was their first kiss?

6. How many children do they want?

7. Where are they going to live?

8. What is their favorite movie?

9. What is their favorite song?

10. What is their favorite activity to do together?

The individual games and activities featured in this section can be used in addition to activities you have planned for your own themed shower, or you can create a themed party around them.

More Wedding Shower Games & Activities

Serve It Up

Hosting a volleyball game is a wonderful idea for a couples' party because it gets everyone involved in the fun. With this game as the basis for your shower, you could have a sports or outdoor theme for the party. Everything you do and include could follow either theme.

Preparation

What You Need

- 3–4 volleyballs

- A volleyball net

- Permanent marking pens

Activity

Set up a volleyball game, dividing couples into two teams. As the game is being played, have each server take two minutes to write a few words of wisdom on the ball with a permanent marker before the ball is served. After the game is over, give the balls to the bride- and groom-to-be. The couple will have a great time reading the advice from their dearest friends.

Wedding Tosses

Let all of the guests feel like a part of the wedding by having everyone make these wedding tosses, which can be passed out after the ceremony to shower the bride and groom with rose petals.

Preparation

What You Need
• 10" paper doilies (have one per guest invited to the wedding)

• Rhinestones in bride's wedding colors

• Silk rose petals

• Staplers with staples

• White glue

Activity
🎁 Roll doilies into a cone shape and staple. Glue a rhinestone over the staple and let dry. Fill the cone with silk rose petals. Store filled cones so they will not be smashed until the wedding day.

More Activities
🎁 Have the bride write her name on three rose petals. Add these three petals to a bowl of plain petals on the table. Have each guest make an additional doily toss for herself. Fill these cones with a few rose petals from the bowl. When the bride opens a guest's gift, the guest tosses her petals on the floor in front of her. If she has a petal with the bride's name, she wins a rose bush to plant in her garden to remember the special day.

Bridal Tray

These bridal trays make a great shower activity as well as a fantastic gift for the bride. While the trays are great for serving, they are also useful as a decorative keepsake to be displayed in the couple's new home.

Preparation

What You Need

• Different-sized picture frames containing a heavy cardboard backing and glass

• Drill and drill bits

• Ephemera, including decorative paper, stickers, photographs, vintage postcards, etc.; or pictures of the bride and groom and other items such as their wedding invitation

• Foam spacers

• Glue or tape

• Handle sets

Activity

Each guest designs and decorates the inside of a frame by adhering ephemera as desired onto cardboard cut to the size of the frame. The ephemera can include saved trinkets that have significance to the couple. Add ribbons, jewels, etc. Using a drill, attach handles onto frames. Place glass, foam spacers, and cardboard into frames and secure the back.

Present each tray to the bride. The bride can later use them as vanity trays for holding perfume, to serve desserts on, or to display.

More Ideas

Trays can be used on the night of the wedding to serve the refreshments.

Each guest could be assigned a different theme for creating their tray. One could be used to serve breakfast, one for tea. One could be filled with memorabilia from the bride's and groom's childhoods or their first date. One could feature the wedding invitations, couples pictures, or match the decor of the couple's new home.

The trays could be a surprise for the bride-to-be. The personal memorabilia may be accessible from the bride without her knowing why, or from her mother or roommate if possible. Be certain to only use copies of important pictures and papers so the originals can be preserved.

Heirloom Quilt

This activity is great for a shower with the bride's family members. Or, invite the groom's family members as well and the quilt can be a creative way to unite the two families in one quilt.

Preparation

What You Need

- Two large pieces of muslin fabric
- Permanent markers
- Straight pins

What To Do Ahead

Ask each guest to bring a piece of clothing to place on the quilt that represents them and the relationship they have with the bride-to-be. For example, Grandpa's shirt or vest pocket, Mom's or Grandma's lacy linen handkerchief, a brother's jean pocket, etc. At the shower have fabric available to lay out the clothing articles.

Activity

Using straight pins, attach clothing items onto the front piece of fabric. Each guest works with the hostess to determine the placement of the item.

On the back piece of fabric, have each guest write a note about the importance of their item and sign it. This should be in alignment with the guest's item on the front piece.

The hostess assembles the quilt after the shower and gives it to the couple as a wedding gift.

Glasses & Coasters

This activity is a great way to involve guests and create a usable keepsake for the bride. Hand-painted glasses will have a special meaning to the bride and groom each time they use them. This activity works well at a couples' shower where each couple can create their own set together to present to the bride and groom. After the newlyweds are settled in their new home, they can invite the shower attendants to visit and use the glasses.

Preparation

What You Need

• 4" clear glass circles or squares available at a stained-glass supply company

• Craft knife

• Cutting board

• Decorative paper, fabric, or photographs

• Felt or flexi-foam

• Glass paint pens to match the couple's decor

• Spray adhesive

• Stemmed glasses

Activity

Glasses

🎁 Have guests hold the glass by the stem and paint their choice of pattern, design, or picture around outside of the glass. Let glasses dry before moving them.

Coasters

🎁 To decorate coasters, spray adhesive onto the patterned side of paper, fabric, or photograph. Place a piece of glass onto the paper. Let dry for a few minutes. Using the craft knife, cut around glass edges to remove excess paper.

Spray adhesive onto one side of felt. Place glass, paper side down, onto felt. Let dry for a few minutes.

Using the craft knife, cut around glass edges to remove excess felt.

Pampering the Bride

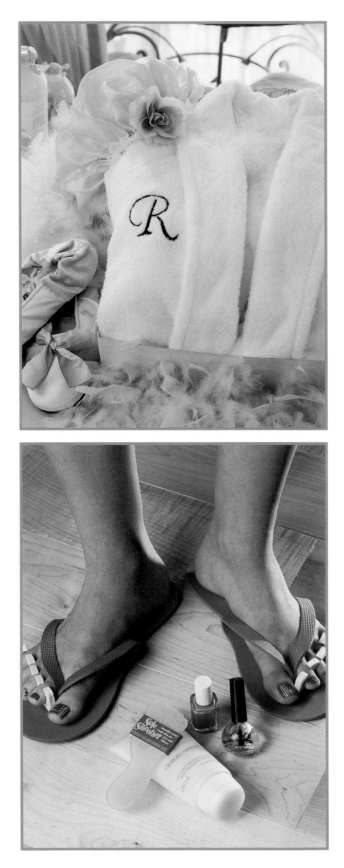

Who does not enjoy being pampered and feeling pretty? At this shower, the guests bring as their gift a product they use to pamper themselves. For example, one may share her favorite brand of perfume, body spray, or makeup product. Another may choose to bring a scented candle or neck massager.

Preparation

What You Need
• A warm, comfortable room large enough for guests to all fit in comfortably

Activities

As each gift is opened, it is passed around the group while the gift giver tells why this relaxes her and the specifics such as different fragrances, styles, and where to purchase the product.

Have additional beauty and pampering supplies on hand for the guests to sample for themselves different products they may not have tried before.

Hire a makeup artist or nail technician to either give the bride-to-be a makeover or to give guests health and beauty tips, a moisturizing treatment, or a simple manicure or pedicure.

I'm at the Wrong Party

This requires an individual who is a good actress and who the rest of the guests do not know. Before the party, provide her with a wedding gift, a fake invitation with a similar address and a purse with the usual purse items inside as well as a few unusual items: comb, wallet, lipstick, tissues, car keys, remote control, etc. Be certain you have a list of the items in the purse. Have her come in as a guest.

Preparation

What You Need

• 20 items to fit in the purse such as:
the shower invitation, store coupon, nail clippers, tissues, safety pin, snack, cell phone, aspirin, keys, address book, picture of a movie star with lipstick marks, colored pencil, scissors, spool of thread, cheap watch, shopping list, yo-yo, comb, wallet, lipstick, remote control, rabbit's foot

• Copies of What Was in My Purse? worksheet on page 53

Activity

Once everyone has arrived, have guests introduce themselves and their relationship to the bride until you get to the "planted" guest. During this time, your "planted" guest can appear to be agitated, nervous, and embarrassed.

Your planted guest will then start stammering and pulling out her invitation, saying she may be at the wrong shower and have her read off the address. She'll jump up embarrassed and flustered and accidentally spill her purse. Be certain she makes a big deal about putting the items back into the purse. Do not have her reclaim her gift. Give a prize to whoever notices first that she did not take her gift.

After she leaves and everyone settles down, hand out the "What Was in My Purse?" worksheets. Ask the guests to write down everything that fell out of the stranger's purse. The one with the most correct answers wins.

Prizes

The prize can be the actual purse and/or the items inside. Be certain the winner knows the purse and the items inside it are new.

Copy this worksheet so there are enough for each guest attending the shower. Provide pens for filling in the answers.

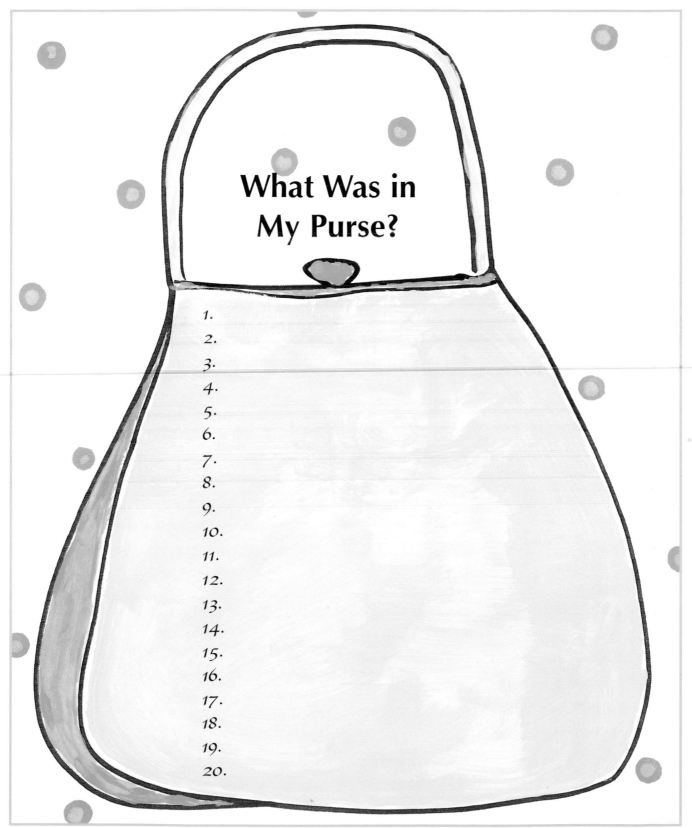

What Was in My Purse?

1.
2.
3.
4.
5.
6.
7.
8.
9.
10.
11.
12.
13.
14.
15.
16.
17.
18.
19.
20.

Takes the Cake

Duplicating the bride's wedding cake or making up your own design makes a great gift card box for the wedding reception.

Preparation

What You Need

- A glue gun and glue sticks

- A paintbrush

- A round box with lid

- A wooden dowel

- Copies of What Cake Is It? worksheet on page 55

- Embellishments: silk flowers, beads, etc.

- Small pieces of handmade paper

- White acrylic paint

- White ribbon rolls, various patterns and sizes

Activities

🎁 Have a work table for guests when they arrive. Have two or three guests create the bottom layer of a wedding cake by painting the box and lid and let dry. They will then pierce the dowel through the box lid and stack ribbon rolls onto the dowel to resemble a wedding cake. They will glue rolls together and let dry. Then they will glue the rolls onto the box lid and let dry. Have them embellish the cake and let dry completely before lifting the lid.

While the cake is being made, give each of the other guests a small piece of handmade paper and assign them a different wedding anniversary: one guest will be the first wedding anniversary, one guest will be the second anniversary, etc. On the paper, have the guest write a wish to the bride and groom for their anniversary. In the box, each guest can place her wish and the bride can read one note on each of her anniversaries. Inside the box, the bride also can place pieces of her wedding memorabilia.

🎁 Play the What Cake Is It? game. Hand out the "What Cake Is It?" worksheets. Ask the guests to write down the answers to the questions about cakes. The one with the most correct answers wins.

Answers: 1. birthday, 2. banana, 3. angel food, 4. cheese, 5. pancake or coffee, 6. cupcake, 7. sponge, 8. date, 9. pound, 10. devil's food, 11. sheet, 12. patty, 13. chiffon, 14. carrot, 15. crab

Copy this worksheet so there are enough for each guest attending the shower. Provide pens for filling in the answers.

What Cake Is It?

1. What cake is an annual event?

2. What cake does a monkey like?

3. What cake has a heavenly body?

4. What cake does a mouse like best?

5. What cake is a typical American breakfast?

6. What cake goes well on a saucer?

7. What cake is found on the ocean floor?

8. What cake is always on a calendar?

9. What cake weighs the most?

10. What cake is the opposite of question #3?

11. What cake should be eaten in bed?

12. What cake is a small child's game?

13. What cake is as lovely as a transparent material?

14. What cake do you feed your rabbit?

15. What cake do you order at a seafood restaurant?

Childhood Memories

A perfect party when inviting childhood friends or family members. Nothing is more touching than sharing old memories and experiences with friends one has known for years. Stories that were not funny at the time, now bring a smile to the face, and the heartache that was shared by a group of friends reminds them of how they learned to comfort one another.

Preparation

What You Need

• Items from the past

Activities

Decorate the party room with memorabilia from the past. Ask guests to come dressed in clothing from an era of the past. Have guests bring old photographs and memorabilia to talk about. Have them also bring some sort of "retro" gift for the couple.

Show school pictures to see who can name the most old school chums.

Play "truth or dare" or a game you would have played from your childhood.

Rice Hunt

This is an activity your guests can get their hands into. You can personalize the game by coloring the rice to match the wedding colors.

Preparation

What You Need

- A blindfold
- A container
- Food coloring (desired color)
- Paper towels
- Rings to hide
- Regular uncooked rice

What To Do Ahead

Add ½ tsp of food coloring to 1 cup water. Pour in desired amount of rice. The longer the rice is left in the water the darker the color will become.

Drain and lay rice out on a paper towel until dry. Place dry, colored rice in container. Hide rings in the rice.

Activities

 In turn, blindfold each guest. Lead them to the container. Time each guest to see who can find all the rings in the fastest time. To make the game a bit more difficult, have the guest wear gloves, too.

 Give each guest a recipe and ingredients for making the colored rice. Have each guest make a batch of rice so the bride has enough for guests to throw after the wedding ceremony.

Prizes

 A nice prize would be a rice cooker.

Worksheets for Wedding Shower Games

Copy this worksheet and have it available to read at a couples' party.

Getting to Know You

Have each woman sit on her husband's lap. Read the questions one at a time. If a guest can answer yes to the question, he/she moves one seat to the right. If the seat is already taken he/she sits on the lap or laps of whoever is already there.

- I am wearing shoes that tie.
- I am wearing a watch.
- I have a button.
- I went to church on Sunday.
- I kissed my sweetie today.
- I am wearing heels.
- I am wearing a ring.
- I have a daughter.
- I am wearing yellow.
- I made my bed this morning.
- I have a zipper.
- I am wearing pants.
- I have a son.

- I have green eyes.
- I like to eat zucchini.
- I have been out of the USA.
- I own a DVD player.
- I drive an SUV.
- I like to ski.
- I listen to country music.
- I have made a soufflé before.
- I have eaten anchovies before.
- I can change a flat tire.
- I have a cat.
- I sleep with my socks on.
- I planted flowers this year.

Before the party, call the groom to get his answers to the following questions. Copy this worksheet so there are enough for each guest attending the shower. Provide pens for filling in the answers.

How Well Does the Groom Know the Bride?

Answer the following questions how you think the groom said the bride would answer.

1. What is the bride's mother's maiden name?

2. Where did the bride and groom have their first date?

3. What is the bride's favorite movie?

4. If the bride were spending an evening at home, what would she most likely be doing?

5. What was the bride's first impression of the groom?

6. Did she ever think she would be marrying him?

7. Where would the bride prefer to live?

8. Where did the groom propose to the bride?

9. What color shirt was the bride wearing when he proposed?

10. When is the bride's mother's birthday?

11. Where was their first kiss?

12. Where did the bride go to high school?

13. What is the bride's favorite food?

14. What is the couple's song?

15. How many children do the couple want?

Ask each guest to bring what she wears in bed in a plain, brown paper bag. As guests arrive, collect the bags. Copy this worksheet so there are enough for each guest attending the shower. Provide pens for filling in the answers. Have guests guess which nightie belongs to whom and cast their votes for the "most" categories.

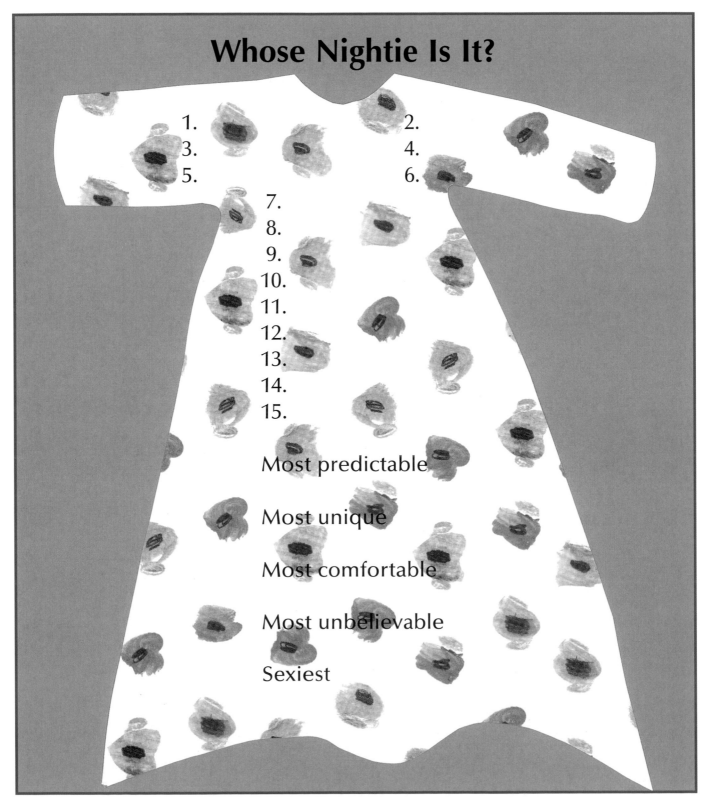

Whose Nightie Is It?

1.
2.
3.
4.
5.
6.
7.
8.
9.
10.
11.
12.
13.
14.
15.

Most predictable

Most unique

Most comfortable

Most unbelievable

Sexiest

Copy this worksheet so there are enough for each guest attending the shower. Provide pens for filling in the answers.

Famous Couples

Fill in the missing husband, wife, or show.

Archie		All in the Family
	Lucy	I Love Lucy
Ralph	Alice	
	Marge	Simpsons
Aladdin		Aladdin
Boris	Natasha	
	June	Leave It to Beaver
Mike	Carol	
Chandler	Monica	
	Joni	Happy Days
Sam		Cheers
Ozzie	Harriet	
	Wilma	The Flintstones
George		The Jeffersons
Heathcliff	Claire	
	Laura	General Hospital
George		The Jetsons
Thurston		Gilligan's Island

Baby Showers

Celebrate the letter "P" as in pink for the mom expecting a girl. If the mother-to-be is having a boy or twins, the theme would be "B" or "T."

Initial Shower

Preparation

What You Need

• Copies of I Spy Something That Begins with the Letter "P" worksheet on page 69

• Decorations as described on page 66

• Food and drinks listed in the Menu on page 67

• Invitation supplies as described on page 66

Crown Pattern

Invitation

🎁 Copy the Crown Pattern at right onto the bottom half of a rectangular card. Run a line of glue around the pattern and cover with glitter to add the sparkle. Fold the card in half vertically. On the inside, copy the following:

For:

Date:

Time:

Place:

   Please Participate, It will be Perfect! Wear something that begins with a "P" such as purple shorts, paisley skirt, or a polka-dot dress. Bring a present that begins with "P" such as patent leather shoes, puffy pink party dress, plush puppy, or a pair of pajamas with a pacifier.

🎁 If the baby has already arrived, invite guests to bring along their small children dressed in "P" clothing as well.

Decorations

🎁 Decorate with everything beginning with your chosen initial. In this case everything is "P." Pink is the color—use only pink, white, or clear glass containers and dishes. Use a parasol to hold pastries, strategically place precious pink pigs and poodles around the party rooms, place primroses on the serving table, use pink polka-dot paper-wrapped pails to hold pirouline cookies, popcorn, and pretzels—whatever you can think of that starts with "P."

🎁 Pears with pineapple wedges and tiny pink parasols paired with pink peanut cups and presented on a pedestal create a colorful centerpiece. Provide peanut-butter cups and a parade of pink marshmallow Peeps for guests to piece on before eating.

Menu

Petite Pepperoni Pizzas

Picture Perfect Parmesan Puree Pesto Pasta

Pistachio Prize Pastry Pudding Pies

Pink Peppermint Paradise Punch

Pretty Peewee Polka-dot P-party Cookies

Peppermint & Peanut Packed Pastel Cups
(cups full of pistachios, peanuts, peppermints,
peach candies, pretzels, and pine nuts)

Pretty Peewee Polka-dot P-party Cookies

3 c sifted flour

1½ tsp baking powder

½ tsp salt

1 c white sugar

1 c butter

1 egg, lightly beaten

3 Tbl cream

1 tsp vanilla extract

Preheat oven to 400 degrees.

In a large bowl, sift together flour, baking powder, salt, and sugar. Cut in butter and blend with a pastry blender until mixture resembles cornmeal. Stir in lightly beaten egg, cream, and vanilla. Blend well. Chill the dough if desired.

On floured surface, roll out dough to ⅛" thickness. Cut into "P" shapes. Transfer to ungreased baking sheets.

Bake 6 to 8 minutes until delicately brown. Let cool, then frost with white frosting and add pink polka dots with pink frosting.

Activity

🎁 From gifts to food and decorations to clothing, this party is filled with "P" words. Give each guest an "I Spy Something That Begins with the Letter P" worksheet. During the shower have each guest list as many Ps as she can find. After the gifts are opened, award a prize to the guest with the most Ps listed.

Prizes & Favors

🎁 Give prizes beginning with the letter "P," such as a purse, picture frame, or perfume.

🎁 Set a timer for a secret amount of time to count down while the new mom is opening her gifts. When the timer rings, whoever gave the gift being opened at the time wins a prize.

Copy this worksheet so there are enough for each guest attending the shower. Provide pens for filling in the answers.

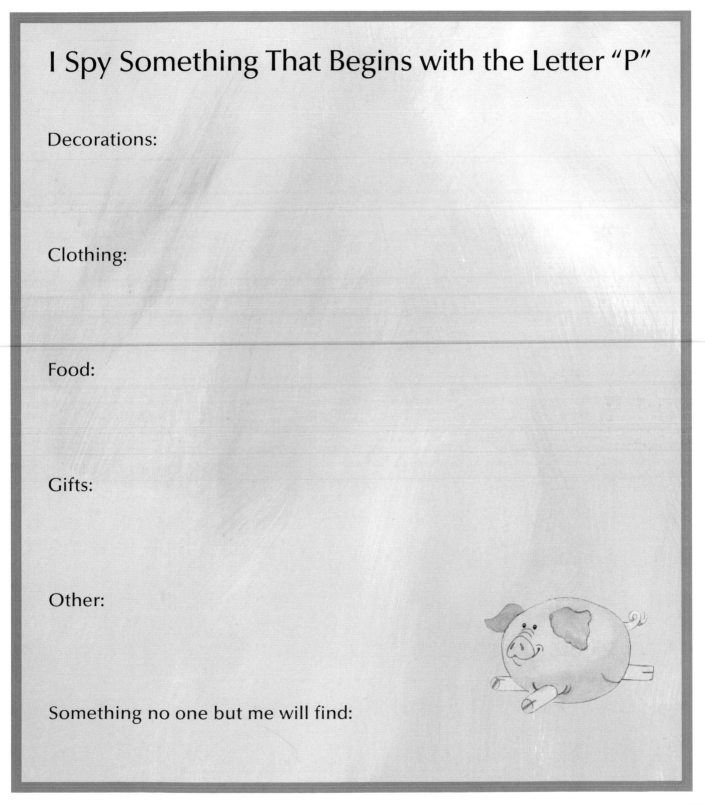

I Spy Something That Begins with the Letter "P"

Decorations:

Clothing:

Food:

Gifts:

Other:

Something no one but me will find:

Having a baby girl is the perfect "happily ever after" for any couple. This shower is a magical way to welcome a new little princess.

Fairy-tale Princess

Preparation

What You Need

- A book made up of fairy-tale pictures

- A calligraphy pen

- Decorations as described on page 72

- Favor supplies as described on page 75

- Food and drinks listed in the Menu on pages 72–73

- Invitation supplies as described on page 72

- Large frame with light-colored mat

- Video camera

What To Do Ahead

Ask one of the guests to come dressed as a fairy godmother and be prepared to lead the telling of a fairy tale.

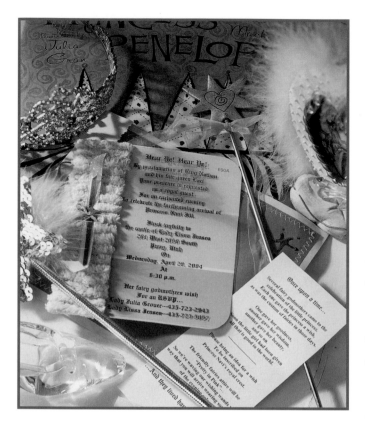

Invitation

🎁 Copy the following text onto vellum, masking off the words in parentheses, and write in the specific information in the spaces provided:

Here Ye! Here Ye!

By proclamation of King (father's name) and his fair Queen (mother's name) , your presence is requested as a royal guest for an enchanted evening to celebrate the forthcoming arrival of Princess (baby's name) .

(date and time)

Flock joyfully to the castle of Lady (Hostess's name and address).

Her fairy godmother wishes for an RSVP (Hostess's phone number)

Cut out the text to fit over a large pink paint chip and secure with a ribbon and lace.

More Invitation Ideas

🎁 Write the invitation in the form of a fairy tale beginning "Once upon a Time."

Decorations

🎁 Decorate the party rooms with fairy-tale- and castle-themed decorations such as tiaras, magic wands, and glass slippers.

🎁 Set up a baby crib with delicate netting falling down around it. Use it as a place to gather the gifts as guests arrive.

🎁 Create a centerpiece for the serving table by stacking two sizes of round boxes and placing the party cake on top of the stack. Place metal vases filled with Gerbera daisies tied together with organza ribbon to look like topiaries on both sides of the centerpiece.

Menu

Since fairies are particularly fond of sweets, the menu for this party is made up entirely of treats:

Princess Crown Cake

Fairy Godmother Magic Wands

Fairy-tale Fudge

Jiggly Gelatin Crowns

Cinderella Strawberries

Sparkling Princess Punch

Sparkling Princess Punch

8 oz. peach nectar

2 c orange juice

2 c cranberry juice

Combine all ingredients and stir. Serve in a pitcher fit for royalty.

Other Treats

Decorate gelatin-shaped crowns with jeweled candies, create edible magic wands using star-shaped cookies and peppermint sticks, and transform a round cake into a crown by frosting sugar cones and arranging them in a circle on the top layer.

73

🎁 Have guests take a turn writing a fairy wish for the baby on the framed picture mat. Make certain they sign their name, too. At the end of the shower, give it to the mother-to-be so that she can insert a photograph of the new baby.

Activities

🎁 With the videotape recording, the fairy godmother begins telling a personalized fairy tale by holding up the picture book and saying, "Once upon a time…" In turn, each guest contributes to the story and subsequently shapes the path it takes—with a happily-ever-after ending, of course. The story may be funny, tender, silly, or adventurous.

After the shower, transcribe the story into the picture book with calligraphy and present it to the new mom.

More Activities

🎁 An alternative to having guests merely tell the fairy tale is to have them act it out while the videotape is recording. Provide various costumes for guests to take on a determined role in a story that is developed before the shower. The characters can include the princess, the queen, the king, the fairy godmother, a cruel witch, a helpful maiden, a dragon, etc.

🎁 Turn the Princess Crown Cake into a prop for playing a game. While decorating the cake, place inside each cone a piece of paper with a written suggestion. During the party, have each guest remove a cone and read aloud what is written. The suggestion may be an act of service to perform for the new mom, such as taking her to the salon during the week, or a silly request such as "do 10 jumping jacks while singing."

🎁 Suggest that your guests bring a gift item that reflects the theme of the party and has something to do with being a princess. Before the honoree opens each gift, have her bestow a wish upon the guest whose gift she is about to open.

🎁 Present a special gift to remind the mom that her precious baby came to be "all because two people fell in love…"

Favors

🎁 Make magic wand party favors. Purchase one large candy-filled straw for each guest. Cut out two stars for each wand from metallic paper. Glue stars together with one or two curly twigs sandwiched between each pair. Let dry overnight.

🎁 Give each guest a sparkling tiara to wear during the party and to take home to remind them that all girls are princesses.

This is a perfect shower to celebrate baby's first Christmas, whether she is born in December or at any other time of the year.

Baby's First Christmas

Preparation

What You Need

- Ball ornaments

- Decorations as described on page 78

- Food and drinks listed in the Menu on page 78

- Glitter glue, paint pens, and permanent marking pens

- Invitation supplies as described on page 78

- Small Christmas tree

Baby's First Christmas

Invitation

🎁 Copy the artwork above onto the right side of a paper cut twice as wide as the card front. Fold the paper into a card. On the inside, copy the invitation information below:

A baby is a Christmas wish come true!

For:
Date:
Time:
Place:

Help us deck the halls to welcome the tiny bundle of joy. Please bring a homemade ornament to present to the new mom.

Menu

Christmas Tree Crackers

Pinecone Cheese Spread

Turkey and Cranberry Baby Cradle Wraps

Angel Food Cake

Holiday Lemonade

Turkey & Cranberry Baby Cradle Wraps

1 lb turkey breast, thinly sliced

½ c walnuts

¼ c cranberries

¼ c extra virgin olive oil

¼ c fresh lemon juice

Salt

Endive leaves (nice big pieces)

Lay turkey on piece of endive leaf. In food processor combine nuts, oil, lemon juice, and salt to taste. Process until a smooth cream forms. Spoon dressing over the turkey, then garnish with walnuts and cranberries.

Decorations

🎁 Use your own Christmas decorations. Remember to bring out the Christmas linens and dishes as well.

Activities

🎁 Have guests give the new mom the ornaments they brought with their gifts.

🎁 During the shower have each guest decorate an ornament, using paint pens, glitter glue, or permanent markers. Be certain guests sign and date the back of the ornaments. Let ornaments dry completely.

As the new mom is presented with each ornament, have a small Christmas tree available for her to hang them on. Supply a pink tree to match a shower for a baby girl or a white tree for a little boy. Let the mom take the tree home with all the ornaments on it.

More Activities

🎁 Have guests write a wish on a decorative tag and attach it onto the ornament. Purchase premade tags, photocopy one of the tags below, or make your own tag design.

🎁 Have an ornament exchange. Each guest brings enough homemade ornaments for everyone. At the end of the shower each guest takes home a number of precious ornaments to adorn their tree.

🎁 Have a cookie exchange as part of the shower. Ask each guest to bring her favorite cookie recipe printed out as well as the cookie in the shape of an ornament prepared for the guests to sample.

This couples' shower combines a new father's favorite hobby with his new role. This is a fun way to welcome dad to the world of babies.

New Dad's Golf Outing

Preparation

What You Need

• A posterboard

• Copies of New Dad's Matching Game photo cards on pages 84–85

• Decorations as described on page 82

• Food and drinks listed in the Menu on page 83

• Invitation supplies as described on page 82

What To Do Ahead

Reserve a room for the shower at the local golf course clubhouse.

Cut the New Dad's Matching Game photo cards apart, excluding the labels. Randomly attach the cards onto a posterboard.

Golf Shirt Patterns

Sleeve

Sleeve

Back

Collar

Collar

Side

Strip

Side

Bottom

Bottom

Inside

Invitation

🎁 Enlarge the Golf Shirt Patterns 250%. Cut Back out of heavy cardstock. Cut Inside out of white paper. Fold inward on dotted lines. Center and glue Inside on top of Back.

Cut Sides and Strip out of newspaper golf clippings. Cut Sleeves and Bottoms out of golf scorecards. Cut Collars out of heavy blue paper. Assemble and glue shirt parts on top of the folded white copy paper. Hot-glue buttons down center.

On the inside, copy the following:

We're hitting the links
to welcome the new little champion!

For:

Date:

Time:

Place:

Decorations

🎁 Create a centerpiece for each table by placing small white flowers in mugs shaped like golf balls. Arrange golf-ball-shaped candies on tees in a tray of lemongrass. Use white and clear glass dishes for serving.

"Baby" Back Barbecue Ribs

"Hole in One" Cheesy Potatoes

"Fore" Sure Baked Beans

"Slice" of Lemon Meringue Pie

"Golf Ball" Cream Puff

"Caddy" Cake

Fresh "Green Tee" Cooler

"Slice" of Lemon Meringue Pie

⅓ c cornstarch

⅛ tsp salt

1¼ c sugar

4 eggs, separated

1 Tbl butter, diced

Grated zest of 1 large lemon

½ c fresh lemon juice (2 or 3 lemons)

Prebaked pie crust

¼ tsp cream of tartar

In a medium saucepan, combine cornstarch, salt, and ¾ cup sugar. Gradually stir in water and bring to a boil over medium heat, stirring constantly, until the mixture thickens. Boil for one minute more.

In a small bowl, beat the egg yolks. Stir in a little of the hot cornstarch mixture, then stir the egg mixture back into the cornstarch mixture in the saucepan and return to heat. Cook over medium-low heat, stirring constantly and rapidly to prevent lumping for about two minutes, until thick. Remove from heat and beat in the butter, then gradually stir in the lemon zest and juice and pour into a prebaked pie crust.

In a medium bowl, using an electric mixer, beat egg whites and cream of tartar until soft peaks form. Sprinkle in the remaining ½ cup of sugar, one tablespoon at a time, beating well after each addition, until the whites form stiff peaks and the sugar is completely dissolved. Test it by rubbing a small amount between your thumb and index finger—it should feel smooth not gritty.

Spoon the meringue onto the warm lemon mixture, spreading to the edge of the crust. Bake for 10 minutes at 375 degrees until the meringue is just golden. Cool completely on wire rack. Best if served the same day.

Activities

Play New Dad's Matching Game. Give each guest a sheet of paper and a pencil. Have them look at the photos on the posterboard and match a "before becoming a dad" item with a "new dad" item. For example, a golf bag and a diaper bag are a match. The guest with the most correct matches wins a prize.

Reserve a tee time and play a couples round of golf or let the men play nine holes while the women enjoy the opening of the gifts and begin eating lunch.

Prizes & Favors

Fill a golf ball basket, such as those found at a driving range, with golf balls, a golf magazine, and various golf accessories to give as a prize.

Fill coffee mugs with bags of golf tees to use as favors for each guest.

New Dad's Matching Game

Dad's Iron

New Dad's Iron

Dad's Rock

New Dad's Rock

Dad's Fore

New Dad's Four

Dad's Bag

Dad's Hole-in-One

Dad's Head Covers

New Dad's Bag

New Dad's Hole-in-One

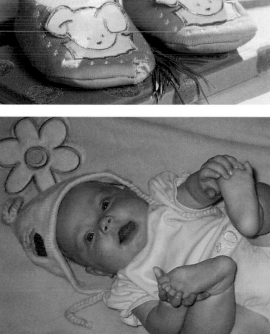

New Dad's Head Cover

85

A honey bee shower is a great way to celebrate the new "bee bee." Bee games and lots of yellow and black will guarantee a "honey" of a time.

A Bee Bee Shower

Preparation

What You Need

- A quart jar

- A timer

- Copies of Honey Bee Trivia and Honey Bee Word Search worksheets on pages 89 and 91

- Decorations as described on page 88–89

- Food and drinks listed in the Menu on page 88

- Invitation supplies as described on page 88

- Paper

- Pencils

- Plastic craft bees

"What's all the buzz?"

Menu

Garden Bee Bee Salad

Honey Cream-filled Crescents

Bumble Bees Honey-glazed Carrots

"Bee Mine" Vanilla Pudding

Golden Honey Nectar

"Bee Mine" Vanilla Pudding

26 chocolate wafers

4 c cold milk

1 large pkg of vanilla instant pudding

Yellow food coloring

8 black gumdrops

Black string licorice

Crush 10 chocolate wafers. Pour milk into a bowl add the instant pudding. Add one drop of yellow food coloring. Beat with a wire whisk until well blended. Spoon one third of the pudding evenly into eight clear parfait dishes. Top each with 1 Tbl of the crushed wafers. Continue layering as follows: pudding, wafers, pudding, wafers, pudding. Refrigerate at least one hour until ready to serve.

Prior to serving, decorate top of layered pudding to resemble a bee by inserting two chocolate wafers for the "wings" and adding a black gumdrop for his face. Use black string licorice for antennae on the gumdrop.

Invitation

📦 Copy the artwork above onto paper twice as wide as the cover, then fold the paper into a card. On the inside, copy the following:

You're invited to a "bee bee" shower to herald the upcoming arrival of   and   's new little honey. Come celebrate a Beeloved Baybee Beeginning with us.

Date:

Time:

Place:

RSVP:

Decorations

📦 Fill the party rooms with all sorts of bees, beehives, honey pots, and yellow and black accessories.

🎁 Purchase or make a large bee-shaped piñata for the centerpiece. Hang bees on a framed piece of chicken wire, which resembles the shapes found in a honeycomb. Arrange large black block letters to say "Bee Happy." Post bee-related verses around the rooms.

Activities

🎁 These activities play on the idea of being able to say "baby" by saying the word "bee" twice—"bee bee." Play either Honey Bee Trivia or Honey Bee Word Search or both, depending on the amount of time you are allotting at your shower. Hand out the worksheets to each guest. The guest that gets the most correct answers wins each game. Time each activity to keep the pace moving.

Honey Bee Trivia

1. How many flowers must honey bees tap to make one pound of honey?

2. How much honey does the average worker bee make in her lifetime?

3. How fast does a honey bee fly?

4. How much honey would it take to fuel a bee's flight around the world?

5. How many sides does each honeycomb cell have?

6. What state is known as the beehive state?

7. How many wings does a honey bee have?

8. How many flowers does a honey bee visit during one collection trip?

9. How do honey bees "communicate" with one another?

10. What does "super" mean to a beekeeper?

Answers: 1. two million, 2. ½ tsp., 3. 15 mph, 4. 2 Tbls, 5. six, 6. Utah, 7. four, 8. 50–100, 9. dancing, 10. a hive box

🎁 Fill a quart jar with plastic craft bees and place on a table with a sheet of paper and pencil. Have each guest write her name on the paper, guess how many bees are in the jar and write the number next to her name. The person who comes closest without going over, wins.

More Activities

🎁 Fill a yellow-and-black workbelt with items that begin with the letter "B." Leave it out on the table. After a while, remove the workbelt and ask guests to list as many items as they can that were in the belt.

🎁 Fill the bee-shaped piñata with small baby gifts—booties, pacifier, baby spoon, a bib. Let the guests break the piñata and shower the new mom with the gifts.

Prizes

🎁 Give winners a pair of yellow beeswax candles tied with a black ribbon.

Honey Bee Word Search Answers

```
B N P O L L I N A T I O N
K E E Y W R L T V Y F N W
W X E L T G A C L O V E R
E D U S L V T O C R Q K T
Q R I A W Q E L D K L R G
H O N E Y A P O I U F O E
I N E W Y Y X N M L M B S
V E C N I Q M Y O B T E N
E Y T O Y W E W U A D E
O K A G I N E I R G O K L
B U R A B R Z K E W E E W
U J E X X K U G K R A E C
Z O E F S N E D R A G P L
Z S K H N C X J O F F E Q
F O R A G E L I W H U R U
```

Copy this worksheet so there are enough for each guest attending the shower. Provide pens for filling in the answers.

Honey Bee Word Search

Beekeeper
Beeswax
Buzz
Clover
Colony
Comb
Drone
Flower
Forage
Garden
Hexagon
Hive
Honey
Insect
Nectar
Petal
Pollen
Pollination
Queen
Worker

```
B N P O L L I N A T I O N
K E E Y W R L T V Y F N W
W X E L T G A C L O V E R
E D U S L V T O C R Q K T
Q R I A W O E L D K L R C
H O N E Y A P O I U F O E
I N E W Y Y X N M L M B S
V E C N I Q M Y O B T E N
E Y T O Y W E W U A D E I
Q K A G I N E I R G O K L
B U R A B R Z K E W E E W
U J E X X K U G K R A E C
Z O E E S N E D R A G P L
Z S K H N C X J O F F E Q
F O R A G E L I W H U R U
```

The individual games and activities featured in this section can be used in addition to activities you have planned for your own themed shower, or you can create a themed party around them.

More Baby Shower Games & Activities

Super Mom

Most mothers are superwomen. They are expected to multitask while treating each task just as importantly as the rest. Whether she is taking care of a baby, doing chores, or advising someone on the phone, a super mom can manage all three tasks at once with ease.

Preparation

What You Need

- A clothesline
- A large doll
- A phone receiver
- A timer
- Baby clothes

Activity

Have two guests hold up the clothesline. Each guest has one minute to hang as many clothes on the line as she can while holding a large doll and the phone at the same time. The person who hangs the most clothes during the time wins.

More Ideas

Depending on the guests, the articles used in the game could also be used as prizes to take home, assuming the guests are also expecting or have small children who could benefit from the items.

Use gifts received as the items in the game. The toys, clothes, and socks could be the items to be hung on the clothesline.

Use an old-fashioned designer phone receiver to make the game harder because the phone is hard to hold with the ear.

Who Wore What?

Test how observant your guests are with this subtle game.

Preparation

What You Need
• A small basket

• Copies of the Who Wore What? worksheet on page 95

• Pencils

• Safety pins

• Small baby items such as: diaper pin, pacifier with clip, baby ribbon, bib, baby booties, baby mittens, washcloth, rattle, baby bottle, small photo frame, baby charm, cutouts of larger baby items one could not wear such as a baby stroller

Activity

🎁 Place baby items in the basket. As guests arrive, attach an item from the basket to their clothing, using a safety pin. Have guests wear the items until everyone has arrived and had a few minutes to mingle.

Collect the items and let some time pass. Hand out Who Wore What? worksheets and ask guests to write down who was wearing which item. When they are finished, pass around the basket again and have each guest take out the item they were wearing. The person with the most correct answers wins. Collect items and present the basket full of items to the mother-to-be.

More Activities

🎁 If the guests do not know each other very well, you may choose to add to this game as a way to get them to talk to one another. At the beginning of the shower tell them they have 15 minutes to get to know as many guests as they can. After the allotted time, give them a piece of paper and ask them to answer questions such as: What is the first and last name of the guest wearing the baby buggy? How many children does the guest wearing the baby bottle have? What is the relationship between the new mom and the guest wearing the rattle? Cater your list to involve all the guests and make it personal to things that apply to them.

Copy this worksheet so there are enough for each guest attending the shower. Provide pens for filling in the answers.

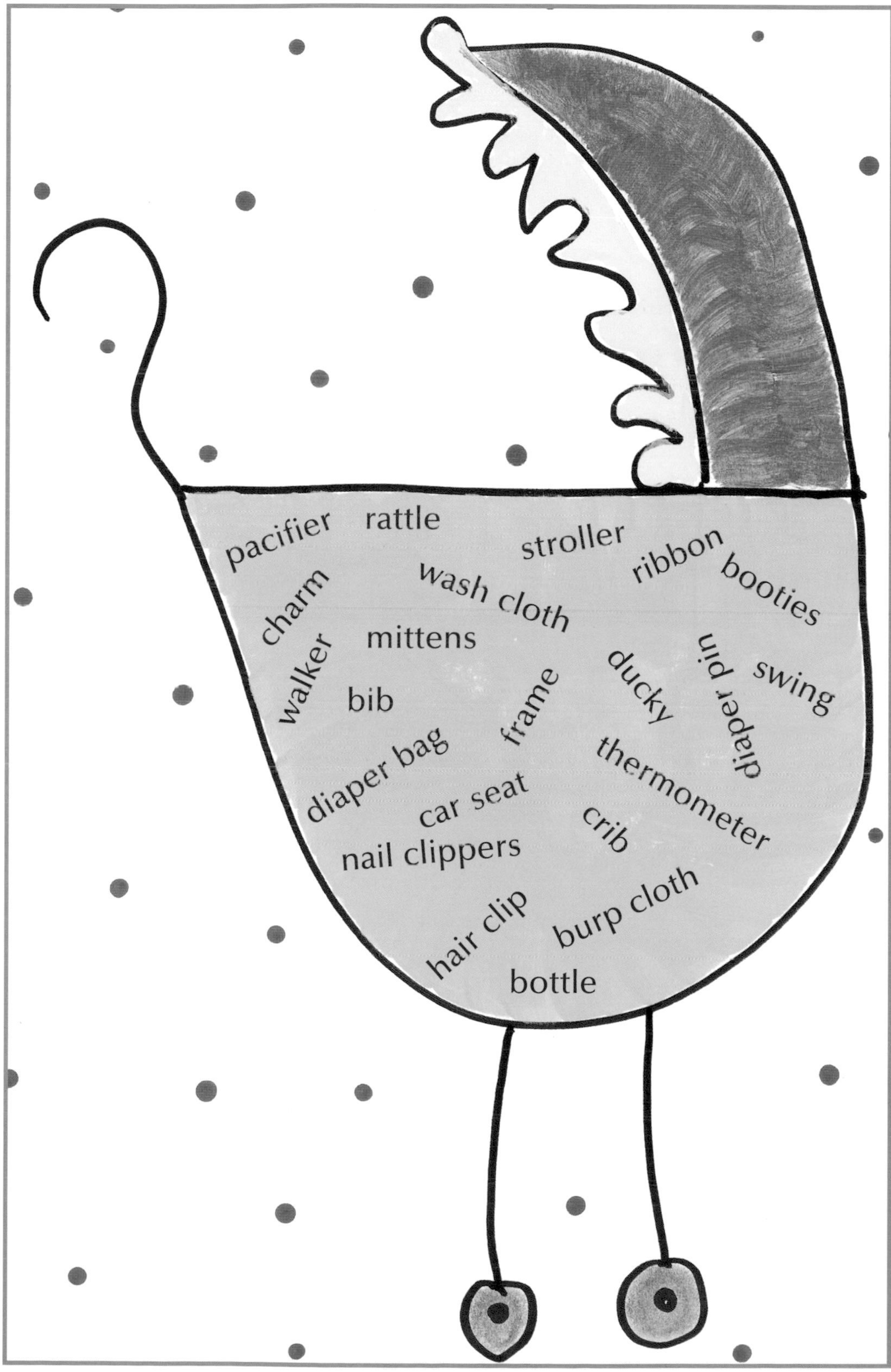

pacifier rattle
stroller ribbon booties
charm wash cloth
walker mittens
bib ducky diaper pin swing
diaper bag frame thermometer
car seat crib
nail clippers
hair clip burp cloth
bottle

Who Wore What?

1.

2.

3.

4.

5.

6.

7.

8.

9.

10.

11.

12.

13.

Stylish Dresser

At a get together for friends, it is always fun to dress up and have an excuse to act silly. This dress-up idea gives plenty of opportunity to do just that.

Preparation

What You Need

• Acrylic paints

• Crazy accessories, about 5 or 6 per guest. You can glean these from your own accessories or go to a thrift store. Use clever ideas—a nice '60s lampshade would make a great hat to wear.

• Large hatboxes, one for each guest

• Ribbon

What To Do Ahead

Paint each box with acrylic paints and allow to dry. Fill each box with the crazy accessories. To include large items, place a note in the box with detailed information as to where the item is hidden. Add a beautiful ribbon—making the box presentation beautiful makes the guests more surprised when they look inside.

Activity

Hand out one box to each guest and tell them to wear whatever is inside. This is a lot of fun and draws a lot of laughs. Have a camera on hand to take photographs of each guest in their outfit. Develop the film and give the photographs to the new mom to send to guests with her thank-you notes.

More Activities

Wrap party prizes and place them in a large hatbox as well. Play a game where guests take turns rolling a pair of dice to get the chance to open one of the prizes. When a guest rolls doubles, she must pass the dice to the next player, quickly put on her accessories, and begin unwrapping one of the prizes—include a pair of gloves in each guest's box to make unwrapping more difficult. If she manages to get the prize unwrapped before another guest rolls doubles, it is hers to keep. If not, she must stop, hand over the prize box, and undress to await another chance to play. The game continues until all of the prizes have been unwrapped.

What's in Your Purse?

The premise for this baby shower activity is the fact that mothers are always prepared.

Preparation

What You Need

• A new purse

• Items that you will want each guest to look for in her purse such as: photograph of a baby, invitation to the shower, pacifier, something pink or blue, eyeglasses, lipstick, grocery coupon, safety pin, nail clippers, spool of thread, candy, baby toy, pen, handkerchief/wet wipe, etc.

• Paper

• Pencils

Activity

Show the purse full of items to the guests. Hand out paper and pencils to guests. One by one, take each item out of the purse and have guests write the names of the items on their paper. Have guests search their own purses for the items on the list. Award one point for each item in the list—the shower invitation is worth an extra five points. The guest with the most points wins a prize.

Present the new purse filled with mom-type items to the new mom so she, too, will always be prepared.

More Activities

Another option is to place a scale on the floor in the middle of the room. Guests will nervously think they might get weighed. However, it is actually to weigh each guest's purse. The guest with the heaviest purse wins a prize.

Prizes

A fun prize idea might be a purse filled with treats. Be prepared to have more than one winner.

Buried in Diapers

This is a great way to help the mom-to-be prepare for her new little one.

Preparation

What You Need
- Curling ribbon
- Transparent tape
- Wide satin ribbon

Activity

🎁 On the invitation, assign a diaper size to each guest, and have them bring a package of diapers in that size. Make certain to assign several guests size 1 to ensure there are enough for the activity. Ask each of them to also bring two small baby items such as toys, socks, spoons, pacifiers, etc.

Have guests work together in three groups to create a three-tiered diaper cake, using 120 size 1 disposable diapers. The bottom tier is made with 50 diapers, the middle with 40 diapers, and the top with 30 diapers.

Open each diaper so it is a long rectangle (keep the sides folded in). Make each tier by starting from the center, rolling up one diaper. Roll the next diaper around it. Continue until you have rolled all diapers in the tier. Use transparent tape to secure the diapers to the

roll as needed. When the tier is complete, wrap a length of curling ribbon around the outside to hold it secure.

Once the tiers are complete, stack them bottom to top. String three 36" pieces of curling ribbon evenly spaced about two-thirds of the way from the center of the top tier down through each tier, catch about two layers of wrapped diapers and string the ribbon back up through the tiers again to the top. Tie the ends together and curl the remaining ribbon ends.

Attach 24" pieces of curling ribbon all around the ribbons used to secure the tiers. Curl all ends and tie small baby toys, socks, spoons, pacifiers, etc. Use wide ribbon to decorate the sides of the cake.

Present the diaper cake and the rest of the diapers to the mom-to-be.

Diving for Diaper Pins

This is an activity your guests can get their hands into. You can personalize the game by coloring the rice pink or blue.

Preparation

What You Need

- A beautiful container
- A blindfold
- A paper towel
- Diaper pins to hide
- Food coloring (desired color)
- Regular uncooked rice

What To Do Ahead

Add ½ tsp of food coloring to 1 cup water. Pour in desired amount of rice. The longer the rice is left in the water the darker the color will become.

Drain and lay rice out on a paper towel until dry. Place dry colored rice in container. Hide the diaper pins in the rice.

Activity

🎁 In turn, blindfold each guest. Lead them to the container. Time each guest to see who can find all the diaper pins the in the fastest time. To make the game a bit more difficult, have the guest wear gloves, too.

Prizes

🎁 After removing the diaper pins and rice, award the winner with the container used for playing this game.

Pacifier Hunt

This activity is centered around the all-important baby's pacifier.

Preparation

What You Need

• An enlarged copy of Pin the Pacifier on the Baby on page 103 and pacifiers below

• Pacifiers

• Tape

Activities

Before guests arrive, hide a number of pacifiers throughout the party room. During the party, explain to the guests that you are having a pacifier hunt. Tell them that a prize will be given for the person who can find the most during the shower.

Play a form of pin the tail on the donkey—but with pacifiers. Secure the enlarged copy of Pin the Pacifier on the Baby to the wall. Blind-fold each guest and have them try to tape a pacifier to the drawing. The pacifier closest to the baby's mouth wins a prize.

More Activities

Add a tag to each hidden pacifier. The tag may indicate that the finder of the pacifier wins a special prize, or that she is obliged to perform an embarrassing act for the other guests, such as jumping jacks, or that she is to perform an act of service for the new mom, such as make her bed or do some shopping for her.

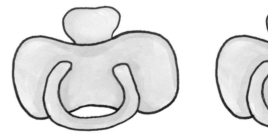

Pin the Pacifier on the Baby

The Price Is Right

This activity is a great way to test your guests' shopping knowledge and get their competitive juices flowing.

Preparation

What You Need

• A brown paper bag

• Copies of The Price Is Right worksheet on page 105

• New baby items to use for the activity: diapers, baby wipes, thermometer, nail clippers, baby comb, baby shampoo, pacifier, bib, socks, diaper cream, undershirt, rattle, baby aspirin, washcloth, outlet cover, baby hanger, etc.

Activity

Place all the baby items in the brown paper bag. Hand out a The Price Is Right worksheet to each guest. In order, take each item out of the bag and have guests guess the retail cost of each item. Display the items so the guests can see them out in the open in case they want to make a price change before the game is over. Have guests tally the grand total. The guest who is closest to the total without going over wins a prize.

Present the expectant mother with the baby items used in the game.

Copy this worksheet so there are enough for each guest attending the shower. Provide pens for filling in the answers.

The Price is Right

1. Diapers $
2. Baby wipes $
3. Thermometer $
4. Nail clippers $
5. Baby comb $
6. Baby shampoo $
7. Pacifier $
8. Bib $
9. Socks $
10. Undershirt $
11. Rattle $
12. Diaper cream $
13. Baby aspirin $
14. Washcloth $
15. Outlet cover $
16. Baby hanger $

Total $

Diaper Bag Surprise

This activity shows how the mom armed with a good diaper bag can carry just about everything but the kitchen sink.

Preparation

What You Need

• A new diaper bag

• 21 baby items

• Copies of Diaper Bag Surprise worksheet below

Activity

Leave baby items out on a table as guests arrive. Have them available for guests to look at. After awhile, take articles away and put them in the diaper bag. Hand out a Diaper Bag Surprise worksheet to each guest and ask them to list the items that were on the table. When they are finished reveal the items again. The guest with the most correct answers wins.

Present the new mom with the filled diaper bag.

Diaper Bag Surprise

1.
2.
3.
4.
5.
6.
7.

8.
9.
10.
11.
12.
13.
14.

15.
16.
17.
18.
19.
20.
21.

Special Delivery

This game is to be played outside. The goal is to keep "your water" from breaking.

Preparation

What You Need

- A bell
- A permanent marking pen
- Paper
- Plastic wrap
- Water balloons

What To Do Ahead

Before the party, write fortunes for guests on scraps of paper predicting what their balloon delivered such as: twins, a boy, a girl, etc. Wrap fortunes in plastic wrap, insert into balloons, then fill the balloons with water. Ask someone not invited to the party to dress in doctor's scrubs and hand out balloons.

Activity

Each guest gets one balloon from the "doctor" at the starting line. Ring the bell. Guests must walk with the balloon between their knees to the finish line. The first guest to make it to the finish line with an unbroken balloon wins.

Prizes

The prize for each fortune should coordinate with the what is written—two of something for twins, something pink for a girl, something blue for a boy, etc.

Picture Perfect

"You've got the cutest little baby face." *See how much everyone has changed by matching up friends and family with their baby pictures.*

Preparation

What You Need

• A baby photograph of each guest with number attached

• A list of all invited guests' names

• A master list of photo numbers matched with names

• Pencils

Activities

On the invitation, ask guests to bring a picture of themselves as a baby. Display the photos in a creative way and assign each a number. Give each guest a sheet of paper and a pencil. Have guests match the number on baby photograph with guest's name. The guest that correctly matches the most, wins a prize.

Arrange several photos of the baby's relatives including the mother, father, grandparents, aunts, and uncles in decorative frames. In one frame, insert a piece of paper with the phrase, "I might look like this when I grow up." Ask guests to identify the relationship of the person pictured to the baby by finding the grandmother, grandfather, etc.

More Activities

If this is a family shower, arrange several photos of the baby's relatives—including the mother, father, grandparents, aunts, and uncles—in decorative frames. See who can name the most relatives. Make it a bit more challenging by displaying pictures of relatives as babies.

Prizes

The guest who correctly guessed the most wins a photo frame.

Baby Bunko

This game requires at least eight players and easily fills an afternoon with friendly competition.

Preparation

What You Need

- A bell
- Copies of Baby Bunko scorecards on page 111
- Pencils
- Three sets of dice
- Tables and chairs

Activity

Set up tables with four chairs each. Pass out scorecards and begin the game. Award prizes for: the most Baby Bunkos, most Baby Buggies, most points, and least points.

Bunko Rules

A game consists of six rounds. The first round rolls to get 1s, the second 2s, etc. The object is to roll more of that round's number than another player at your table. To begin, the mom-to-be rings a bell. The first person on each team starts rolling the dice. As long as they get at least one of that round's number on any of the three dice, they keep rolling. If not, the dice are passed to the player at the left. As soon as someone gets 21 points, the round ends. The person with the most points at each table moves to a new table to start again.

Scoring

Each player keeps her own score. One point is awarded for each of that round's number rolled. For example, in the first round you are rolling for 1s. You roll a 1, a 6, and a 2. You score one point and keep rolling—use the large box on column one, row one to write down points as they are rolled. On the next roll, you roll a 3 and two 1s. You score two points and continue to roll. On the next roll, you get two 5s and a 3—you score no points and pass the dice. If you roll three-of-a-kind, but not of that round's number, it is worth 5 points. But, you do not continue rolling. This is called a "Baby Buggy." Keep track of your Baby Buggies. If three-of-a-kind is rolled and it is that round's number, it is an automatic "Baby Bunko." The person yells "Baby Bunko" and rings the bell. They receive 21 points for the Baby Bunko, plus whatever other points they received in that round. All guests then tally their points from the first round and write the number in the smaller box on the first column, first row.

At the end of the first round, place your grand total on the small line under the first column. Keep track of any Baby Buggies or Baby Bunkos. You now move on to round two and keep score down the second column. Repeat the process for remaining rounds. When the game is over, total all five rows and write the number on the double line at the bottom-right corner.

Copy this scorecard so there are enough for each guest attending the shower. Provide pencils for filling in the scores.

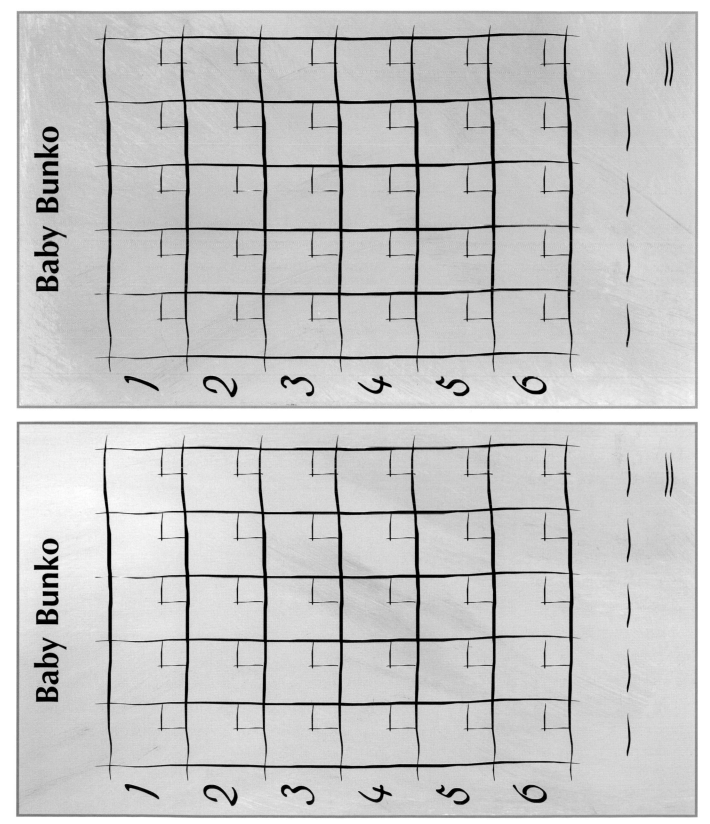

Expecting Baby Bingo

Who doesn't love a rousing game of Bingo? In this adaptation, guests are waiting for baby items to be called instead of numbers.

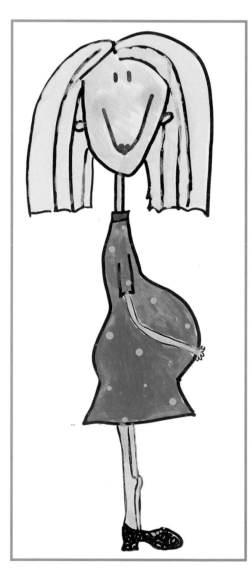

Preparation

What You Need

• Copies of Baby Bingo worksheet on page113

• Pencils

• Something to cover called spaces

Activity

🎁 Hand out a Baby Bingo worksheet to each guest. Instruct the guests to think of common baby items, then have them write those items in each of the squares. The center square is free. The hostess then reads off random baby items. The guests cover the square that has been called by the hostess. The first guest to get five across, five down, or five diagonally wins.

Suggested baby items include: Q-tips, baby quilt, high chair, nursing, rattle, T-shirt, formula, diaper, bib, baby lotion, girl, boy, teething ring, lullaby, diaper bag, nightgown, car seat, stroller, changing table, stuffed animal, baby powder, baby wipes, baby swing, baby vitamins, crib, bassinet, crib sheets, pacifier, baby spoon, baby food, washcloth, booties, cradle, rice cereal, juice, baby bottle, diaper pail, pediatrician, proud parents.

More Activities

🎁 This game also can be played out as the mom-to-be opens her gifts. If the gift matches what the guest has written in one of her spaces, she covers the space.

Prizes

🎁 Reward the efforts of the bingo players with quirky prizes such as a baby bottle filled with candy, a necklace made from colored diaper pins pinned together, or a pint of gourmet ice cream with a jar of pickles.

Baby Bingo

Worksheets for Baby Shower Games

Copy this worksheet so there are enough for each guest attending the shower. Provide pens for filling in the answers.

Baby Scramble

Be the first to unscramble these common items for the baby.

1. OLBETT
2. CAPIEFIR
3. IPDARE
4. BLAYULL
5. CALRED
6. LCBOSK
7. KRCONIG SHORE
8. YSTO
9. RUNSYER HRMEYS
10. EATRLT
11. NKTABLE
12. YLAPNEP
13. RERLTSOL
14. AYBB TNOLOI
15. DWROPE

Answers: 1. bottle, 2. pacifier, 3. diaper, 4. lullaby, 5. cradle, 6. blocks, 7. rocking horse, 8. toys, 9. nursery rhymes, 10. rattle, 11. blanket, 12. playpen, 13. stroller, 14. baby lotion, 15. powder

Copy this worksheet so there are enough for each guest attending the shower. Provide pens for filling in the answers.

Because Mommy Said

Guests compete to find out who is the best "mind reader" as they try to finish mommy's phrase. Have the mommy and each guest fill out a worksheet. When they are all finished, read mommy's answers. The winner is the guest who answers most like mommy.

Example:
Baby_____(Was it baby booties, baby girl, baby wipes?)

1. Tiny_____   7. Warm_____
2. Cute_____   8. Sleepy_____
3. Baby_____   9. Burp_____
4. Diaper_____   10. Chubby_____
5. Changing_____   11. _____Bottle
6. Bath_____

Copy this worksheet so there are enough for each guest attending the shower. Provide pens for filling in the answers.

Baby Parts

1. What you should keep out of other people's business
2. What the tortoise raced with
3. The biggest part of a giraffe
4. Two sailors answering yes
5. When two pipes are joined
6. What you put to the wheel
7. Used on Valentine's Day
8. The edge of a cup or glass
9. What a wrecking car does
10. Something to keep tools in
11. Three heads plus one more
12. Grown on a cornstalk
13. A type of macaroni
14. Used by carpenters
15. Weapons of war
16. Branches of a tree
17. A school child
18. Part of a wagon
19. Tropical trees
20. Part of an apple
21. Edge of a saw
22. Part of a clock

23. What dogs bury
24. Part of a bed
25. Used to cross a river
26. Used to hail a ride
27. What we think with
28. Part of an umbrella
29. Opposite the head
30. Place of worship
31. Weathercocks
32. Part of a river
33. A type of watch
34. Center of celery
35. A young cow
36. Top of a hill
37. A hobo
38. A clam

Answers: 1. Nose, 2. Hair, 3. Neck, 4. Eyes, 5. Joint, 6. Shoulder, 7. Heart, 8. Lip, 9. Toes, 10. Chest, 11. Forehead, 12. Ears, 13. Elbow, 14. Nails, 15. Arms, 16. Limbs, 17. Pupil, 18. Tongue, 19. Palm, 20. Skin, 21. Teeth, 22. Face or Hands, 23. Bones, 24. Head or Foot, 25. Bridge, 26. Thumb, 27. Brain, 28. Ribs, 29. Foot, 30. Temple, 31. Veins, 32. Mouth, 33. Wrist, 34. Heart, 35. Calf, 36. Brow, 37. Bum, 38. Muscle

Copy this worksheet once and cut slips apart. Fold each slip and place in a bowl. Divide guests into two teams. Set the timer for two minutes. A member from the first team chooses a slip and, without making any sounds, acts out the nursery rhyme. His team gets a point for every rhyme it guesses exactly before the timer rings. The second team resets the timer and takes its turn. When all slips are gone the team with the most points wins.

Nursery Rhymes Charades

Ring Around the Rosie	Old King Cole
Georgie Porgie, Puddin' & Pie	Little Jack Horner
Hey Diddle Diddle	Simple Simon Met a Pie Man
Old Mother Hubbard	The Queen of Hearts
Baa, Baa, Black Sheep	Little Miss Muffet
Old Woman/Lived in a Shoe	The House That Jack Built
Jack Be Nimble	One, Two, Buckle My Shoe
Mary, Mary Quite Contrary	There Was a Crooked Man
Jack and Jill Went Up the Hill	Peas Porridge Hot
Little Bo-Peep	Jack Sprat Could Eat No Fat
Sing a Song of Sixpence	Humpty Dumpty
Three Little Kittens	Peter, Peter Pumpkin Eater
Hickory Dickory Dock	Little Boy Blue

Copy this worksheet so there are enough for each guest attending the shower. Provide pens for filling in the answers.

Hidden Words

Hidden in each of the sentences below is a word about the baby, the family, or the baby's needs. To find a hidden word, connect consecutive letters in two or more words. When you find such a word, underline it.

Example: This could be the pitch that wins the game.

1. Everyone knows that children live in fantasy worlds.

2. Could any movie star rival the great Clark Gable?

3. I promised to do Trudi a personal favor this week.

4. Keep eating like that and you will get fat, Herman.

5. When he sees him, Mac ribs Joe about their card game.

6. Pregnant women display penchants for unusual food.

7. The painter advised him to buy the best rollers and brushes.

8. You should chip in so we can buy Susan a present.

9. Hoover Dam has the world's largest dynamo there.

10. He's building a house on the lot I once owned.

Answers:
1. Everyone knows that children live <u>in fant</u>asy worlds.
2. Could any movie s<u>tar rival</u> the great Clark Gable?
3. I promised to do Tru<u>di a per</u>sonal favor this week.
4. Keep eating like that and you will get <u>fat, Her</u>man.
5. When he sees him, M<u>ac ribs</u> Joe about their card game.

6. Pregnant women dis<u>play pen</u>chants for unusual food.
7. The painter advised him to buy the be<u>st rollers</u> and brushes.
8. You should chi<u>p in so</u> we can buy Susa<u>n a present</u>.
9. Hoover Dam has the world's largest dyna<u>mo there</u>.
10. He's building a house on the <u>lot I on</u>ce owned.

118

Copy this worksheet so there are enough for each guest attending the shower. Provide pens for filling in the answers.

Rhyme Time

Answer the questions about the various nursery rhymes referred to below.

1. What time did the mouse run down the clock?

2. What was Wee Willie Winkie wearing?

3. What did Jack Be Nimble jump over?

4. What did the Dish run away with?

5. What kind of pie was Little Jack Horner eating?

6. When Simple Simon met the pie man, where was he going?

7. What was Little Miss Muffett eating?

8. Why did Jack and Jill go up the hill?

9. What followed Mary to school one day?

10. How many days old was the peas porridge in the pot?

11. How many bags of wool did the black sheep have?

12. What couldn't Jack Sprat eat?

13. Where was Little Boy Blue?

14. Where does the Muffin Man live?

15. What did the three little kittens lose?

Answers: 1. one o'clock, 2. his nightgown, 3. the candle stick, 4. the spoon, 5. Christmas or plum, 6. to the fair, 7. curds and whey, 8. to fetch a pail of water, 9. little lamb, 10. nine, 11. three, 12. fat, 13. under the haystack, 14. on Drury Lane, 15. their mittens

How Fast Can You Draw a Baby?

The object of this game is to be the first player to finish drawing a baby. Copy one set of the colored cards below. Copy the How Fast Can You Draw a Baby? worksheet on page 121 so there are enough for each guest attending the shower. Cut cards apart, number them on the back from 1 to 6 and lay them face-down in the center of the playing area.

Each player starts with a pencil and a worksheet. Players take turns rolling a die and then drawing the body part that corresponds to the number rolled. If a player rolls a number she has already completed, she must wait until her next turn and try again. Whoever completes the drawing of "her" baby first wins.

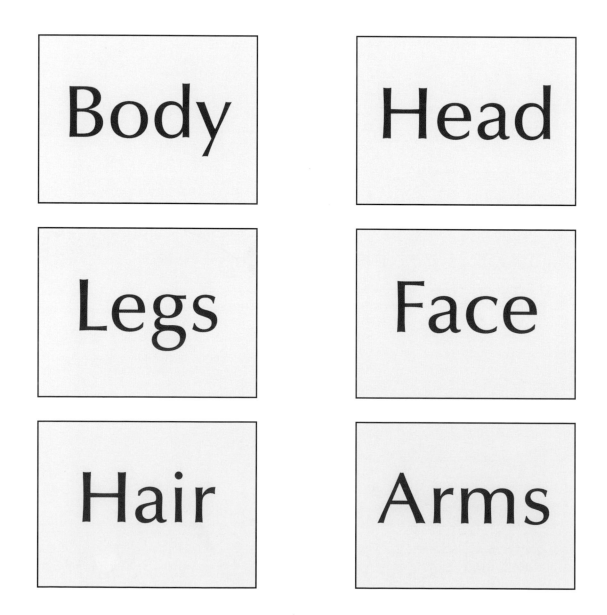

How Fast Can You Draw a Baby?

Noah's Ark

Name an animal, fish, or bird for every letter of the alphabet. The first one done is the winner.

A

B

C

D

E

F

G

H

I

J

K

L

M

N

O

P

Q

R

S

T

U

V

W

X-free space

Y

Z

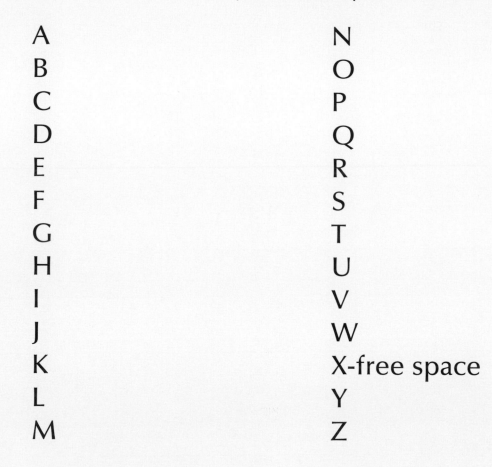

Example answers: A-aardvark, B-bear, C-camel, D-dinosaur, E-elephant, F-fish, G-gopher, H-hamster, I-iguana, J-jackel, K-kangaroo, L-lamb, M-muskrat, N-newt, O-owl, P-platypus, Q-quail, R-rabbit, S-seal, T-turtle, U-unicorn, V-vulture, W-walrus, Y-yak, Z-zebra

How Long Game

Match the animal with the approximate number of days they are pregnant. The one who gets the most right wins.

1. Camel	a. 15	
2. Chicken	b. 21	
3. Cow	c. 22	
4. Deer	d. 30	
5. Dog	e. 33	
6. Duck	f. 51	
7. Elephant	g. 65	
8. Fox	h. 109	
9. Giraffe	i. 115	
10. Goat	j. 139	
11. Hippopotamus	k. 155	
12. Horse	l. 197	
13. Kangaroo	m. 240	
14. Lion	n. 280	
15. Monkey	o. 335	
16. Pig	p. 365	
17. Pigeon	q. 370	
18. Rabbit	r. 450	
19. Whale	s. 455	
20. Zebra	t. 510	

Answers: 1. s, 2. c, 3. n, 4. l, 5. g, 6. b, 7. t, 8. f, 9. r, 10. k, 11. m, 12. o, 13. e, 14. h, 15. j, 16. i, 17. a, 18. d, 19. p, 20. q

'Thank You'

At the end of the shower, the honoree will have a complete list of guests with their addresses, ready-to-mail envelopes, and photographs she can photocopy and send with her thank-you notes.

Preparation

What You Need

- A blank guest book
- A decorative container
- A pen
- A polaroid camera
- Cards and envelopes
- Colored pencils, pens, stickers, etc.

Activities

▥ Have guests sign the guest book and include their address and phone number. Take a photograph of each guest with the shower honoree to use as a keepsake. Send a copy of the photograph with the thank-you card as a memento for the guest.

▥ Have each guest decorate and address an envelope to themselves. Drop all envelopes into the container. During the shower, the honoree can draw out envelopes randomly and give out door prizes to the guests whose envelopes were pulled. After the shower, the honoree has already-addressed envelopes to send thank-you notes in.

More Activities

▥ Photocopy one of the designs below to make your own personalized card.

Special thanks to:

Jo Packham

Laura Best

Leslie Ridenour

Nate, Laci, and Navi Davis

Gisel Nehring

David and Lissa Jensen

Doug and Julia Grover

Jan Tanner

Shelly Reber

Limousine Connection

Heidi Farner

Tyese Christenson

Brenda Christensen

Kristi Williams

Tiffany Burnhope

Josh Thompson

Zak Mudow

Staci Case

Trekker Gray

Angela Gilmore

Richard, Levi, and River Grover

Cindy Stoeckl

Ryne Hazen

Suzy Skadberg

All the staff at Chapelle, Ltd.

About the Author

Jill Grover, an interior designer, is the mother of three and resides with her husband and children in Northern Utah. She has appeared locally as well as nationally on various television programs, sharing advice on crafting and decorations. She has made use of her creative talents as the author of *Scary Scenes for Halloween, Handmade Giftwrap, Bows, Cards, and Tags,* and *Dimestore Decorating* as well as *Throwing the Perfect Shower.* She also plays the harp and makes really great chocolate chip cookies.

Metric Conversion Chart

mm-millimetres   cm-centimetres
inches to millimetres and centimetres

inches	mm	cm	inches	cm	inches	cm
⅛	3	0.3	9	22.9	30	76.2
¼	6	0.6	10	25.4	31	78.7
⅜	10	1.0	11	27.9	32	81.3
½	13	1.3	12	30.5	33	83.8
⅝	16	1.6	13	33.0	34	86.4
¾	19	1.9	14	35.6	35	88.9
⅞	22	2.2	15	38.1	36	91.4
1	25	2.5	16	40.6	37	94.0
1¼	32	3.2	17	43.2	38	96.5
1½	38	3.8	18	45.7	39	99.1
1¾	44	4.4	19	48.3	40	101.6
2	51	5.1	20	50.8	41	104.1
2½	64	6.4	21	53.3	42	106.7
3	76	7.6	22	55.9	43	109.2
3½	89	8.9	23	58.4	44	111.8
4	102	10.2	24	61.0	45	114.3
4½	114	11.4	25	63.5	46	116.8
5	127	12.7	26	66.0	47	119.4
6	152	15.2	27	68.6	48	121.9
7	178	17.8	28	71.1	49	124.5
8	203	20.3	29	73.7	50	127.0

yards to metres

yards	metres	yards	metres	yards	metres	yards	metres	yards	metres
⅛	0.11	2⅛	1.94	4⅛	3.77	6⅛	5.60	8⅛	7.43
¼	0.23	2¼	2.06	4¼	3.89	6¼	5.72	8¼	7.54
⅜	0.34	2⅜	2.17	4⅜	4.00	6⅜	5.83	8⅜	7.66
½	0.46	2½	2.29	4½	4.11	6½	5.94	8½	7.77
⅝	0.57	2⅝	2.40	4⅝	4.23	6⅝	6.06	8⅝	7.89
¾	0.69	2¾	2.51	4¾	4.34	6¾	6.17	8¾	8.00
⅞	0.80	2⅞	2.63	4⅞	4.46	6⅞	6.29	8⅞	8.12
1	0.91	3	2.74	5	4.57	7	6.40	9	8.23
1⅛	1.03	3⅛	2.86	5⅛	4.69	7⅛	6.52	9⅛	8.34
1¼	1.14	3¼	2.97	5¼	4.80	7¼	6.63	9¼	8.46
1⅜	1.26	3⅜	3.09	5⅜	4.91	7⅜	6.74	9⅜	8.57
1½	1.37	3½	3.20	5½	5.03	7½	6.86	9½	8.69

Index